Christin Milloy

Canada's Transgender Trailblazer – Unfiltered

Santiago Gonzalez

ISBN: 9781779696847
Imprint: Telephasic Workshop

Contents

Introduction: Who the Fuck Is Christin Milloy?

Canada's First Transgender Politician: Milloy's Fucking Journey from Activism to Politics

Breaking Through Political Fucking Barriers: How Milloy Entered Canadian Politics as a Transgender Candidate

In this section, we will explore the incredible journey of Christin Milloy as she broke through political fucking barriers to become one of Canada's first openly transgender fucking Candidates. Milloy's determination, passion, and groundbreaking work paved the way for greater transgender representation in Canadian politics.

The Fucking Political Landscape in Canada: Navigating a Fucking System That Wasn't Ready for Her

To understand Milloy's political journey, we first need to grasp the complex and challenging fucking political landscape she entered. At the time, Canadian politics was predominantly male-dominated, lacking diversity and representative voices. The LGBTQ community, particularly transgender individuals, faced significant discrimination and marginalization.

Fucking traditional political parties mostly focused on conservative values, making it difficult for progressive voices to be heard. Transgender issues were often misunderstood, ignored, or even ridiculed. The political system was not ready for someone like Milloy, a transgender woman fighting for equality and justice.

How Milloy Entered Canadian Politics: A Fucking Outrageous Journey

Milloy's entry into Canadian politics was anything but ordinary. Fueled by a desire to bring about meaningful change, she embarked on a fucking outrageous journey that challenged societal norms and shattered glass ceilings.

Milloy recognized the power of political participation in transforming society and saw politics as an avenue for advocating for the rights of transgender individuals. She decided to run as a candidate in a local election, becoming one of Canada's first openly transgender fucking candidates.

The Fucking Impact of Milloy's Candidacy: Inspiring Others to Embrace Their Authenticity

Milloy's candidacy sparked a fucking tidal wave of inspiration, resonating with not only the transgender community but also with individuals from all walks of life. She showed the world that authenticity and self-acceptance were not only possible but also fucking powerful.

By running for office, Milloy brought transgender issues to the forefront and forced the public and other politicians to confront their preconceived notions of gender identity. Her campaign was a radical act of defiance against a system that had long excluded and disregarded marginalized voices.

The Fucking Challenges Milloy Faced: Battling Ignorance and Transphobia

Milloy's journey into politics was not without its share of challenges. She encountered ignorance and fucking transphobia throughout her campaign. Some opponents belittled her, dismissing her as incapable of leadership solely because of her transgender identity.

However, Milloy's resilience and unwavering commitment allowed her to rise above the hate. She took the opportunity to educate the public, debunk stereotypes, and challenge the patriarchal and cisnormative structures that perpetuated discrimination against transgender individuals.

The Fucking Triumph of Milloy's Candidacy: A Major Step Forward for Transgender Representation

Despite the challenges, Milloy's historic candidacy marked a major step forward for transgender representation in Canadian politics. Her campaign brought attention to the unique struggles faced by the transgender community, forcing politicians and lawmakers to acknowledge and address these issues.

Milloy's bold entry into politics helped to break down the fucking barriers blocking transgender voices from being heard. She paved the way for future generations of transgender politicians, showing that they too could aspire to elected office without compromising their authenticity.

The Fucking Impact of Milloy's Candidacy: Inspiring Political Change

Milloy's candidacy had a lasting impact on Canadian politics. It inspired a new wave of activism and political involvement, both within and outside the LGBTQ community. People who had previously felt invisible and unheard found hope and courage in her journey.

Additionally, Milloy's presence in the political arena prompted political parties to reevaluate their approach to inclusivity and diversity. Her campaign pushed for LGBTQ-inclusive policies, forcing politicians from all backgrounds to confront their biases and take steps towards a more equitable and representative political system.

The Future of Transgender Politics in Canada: Milloy's Fucking Work Paving the Way

Milloy's groundbreaking journey into Canadian politics opened doors that had long been closed to transgender individuals. Her advocacy work, courage, and perseverance laid the foundation for future transgender candidates to enter politics and shape the political landscape.

Moving forward, Milloy's legacy serves as a reminder that political participation is essential for advancing transgender rights and achieving social justice. Her work continues to inspire and empower transgender individuals to dismantle barriers, fight for equality, and create lasting change within the political sphere.

Conclusion

Milloy's entrance into Canadian politics as a transgender candidate was a remarkable feat, shattering stereotypes, challenging the status quo, and opening doors for future generations. Her journey demonstrated the power of authenticity and served as a catalyst for change within the political fucking system. Despite the obstacles she faced, Milloy's legacy will forever be remembered as a turning point in transgender representation in Canadian politics.

The Fucking Importance of Milloy's Advocacy: How She Shaped Fucking Transgender Rights in Canada

Christin Milloy's advocacy work has played a critical role in shaping transgender rights in Canada. Through her tireless efforts, she has raised awareness, challenged discriminatory policies, and pushed for legal reforms that have created a more inclusive and accepting society for transgender individuals.

The Fucking Power of Visibility

One of the most significant contributions of Milloy's advocacy is the visibility she has brought to the transgender community. By openly discussing her own experiences and challenges as a transgender person, she has shattered stereotypes and misconceptions. Through her interviews, public speaking engagements, and media appearances, she has shown the world that transgender individuals are diverse, resilient, and deserving of respect and equal rights.

Milloy's visibility has not only humanized the transgender experience, but it has also helped to dispel myths and educate the general public. Her willingness to share personal stories and openly discuss her journey has allowed people to develop a deeper understanding and empathy for the transgender community. This increased visibility has paved the way for greater acceptance and support, changing the conversation around transgender rights in Canada.

Fucking Shaping Legal Reforms

Milloy's advocacy has had a profound impact on the legal landscape in Canada. By highlighting the systemic injustices faced by transgender individuals, she has been instrumental in driving legislative changes that protect transgender rights and promote equality.

One area where Milloy has made a significant impact is in advocating for gender identity recognition. She has been a vocal proponent for allowing individuals to have their gender identity legally recognized without unnecessary medical or legal barriers. Thanks to her efforts, Canada has taken significant steps towards more inclusive gender identification options on government documents such as passports, drivers' licenses, and health cards.

Furthermore, Milloy's advocacy has played a crucial role in the fight against employment and housing discrimination faced by transgender individuals. She has championed the need for comprehensive anti-discrimination laws that protect transgender rights in all areas of life. Her advocacy work has inspired legal reforms that prohibit discrimination based on gender identity and expression, ensuring that transgender individuals have the same opportunities and protections as their cisgender counterparts.

The Fucking Importance of Intersectionality

In her advocacy work, Milloy has consistently emphasized the importance of intersectionality. She has recognized that the fight for transgender rights cannot be separated from the broader struggles faced by marginalized communities. By actively engaging with other LGBTQ advocates, feminists, and racial justice activists, she has fostered coalitions that fight for equality on multiple fronts.

Milloy's intersectional approach to advocacy has addressed the unique challenges faced by transgender individuals who belong to multiple marginalized groups. She has highlighted the disproportionate impact of discrimination and violence on transgender individuals of color, immigrants, and those from low-income backgrounds. By amplifying these voices and advocating for their specific needs, she has worked towards a more inclusive and equitable society for all transgender individuals.

The Fucking Future of Transgender Rights in Canada

Milloy's advocacy has laid a strong foundation for future progress in transgender rights in Canada. Her commitment to visibility, legal reforms, and intersectionality has set a precedent for future activists and advocates.

Moving forward, it is crucial for the fight for transgender rights to continue. While significant strides have been made, there is still work to be done to ensure full equality and acceptance for all transgender individuals. This includes addressing issues such as healthcare access, mental health support, and education on transgender issues.

The legacy of Milloy's advocacy will continue to inspire future generations of activists to challenge societal norms, fight for equal rights, and create a more inclusive Canada for transgender individuals. Through collective action and continued advocacy, the vision of a society where transgender rights are fully recognized and respected can become a reality.

Fighting for Fucking Visibility: How Milloy Became a Fucking Voice for the Transgender Community

In this section, we will explore how Christin Milloy emerged as a powerful voice for the transgender community, fighting for greater visibility and representation. Milloy's journey to becoming a transgender activist was shaped by personal experiences, a deep commitment to social justice, and a desire to create a more inclusive society.

The Fucking Power of Representation

Representation is a powerful tool in creating social change. Seeing individuals who share similar experiences and identities in positions of power and influence can have a profound impact on marginalized communities. By becoming a public figure and openly advocating for transgender rights, Milloy became a beacon of hope and inspiration for countless individuals struggling with their own identities.

Milloy recognized the importance of visibility in challenging societal norms and misconceptions about transgender people. She understood that by being openly transgender herself and confidently sharing her story, she could help break down barriers and foster a more compassionate and accepting society. Milloy's visibility was a catalyst for change, as it allowed others to recognize their own potential and actively engage in the fight for transgender rights.

Creating Fucking Safe Spaces

Milloy began her activism by creating safe spaces for transgender individuals to share their experiences, seek support, and build a sense of community. Through organizing events, support groups, and online platforms, she provided a platform for transgender people to express themselves authentically.

By fostering these safe spaces, Milloy empowered transgender individuals to find their voice and assert their rights. She created an environment where people could learn from each other, gain confidence, and challenge societal prejudices. These safe spaces became a crucial part of Milloy's advocacy work, as they not only provided support but also served as a platform for voicing the concerns and experiences of the transgender community.

Amplifying Fucking Transgender Voices

Milloy believed in the power of storytelling as a means of creating understanding and empathy. She recognized that by sharing personal stories and experiences, transgender individuals could humanize the struggles they face and change public perception.

To amplify transgender voices, Milloy used various media platforms to raise awareness about transgender issues. She wrote articles, gave interviews, and used social media to engage with a wide audience. Milloy's ability to articulate the challenges, triumphs, and everyday experiences of the transgender community played a significant role in shifting public opinion and generating support for transgender rights.

Forging Alliances and Fucking Building Coalitions

As an advocate for transgender rights, Milloy understood the importance of building alliances and coalitions with other LGBTQ activists and supporters. She recognized that by working together, they could amplify their collective voices and effect greater change.

Milloy actively collaborated with LGBTQ organizations, human rights groups, and other social justice advocates. By establishing connections and partnerships, she was able to pool resources, reach a broader audience, and influence policymakers. Importantly, these collaborations helped bridge gaps and unite advocates from different backgrounds, fostering solidarity and building a more inclusive movement.

Fucking Social Media as a Tool for Change

Utilizing the power of social media, Milloy harnessed online platforms to engage with people, share information, and challenge misconceptions. She recognized that social media had the potential to democratize activism and reach a global audience.

Milloy embraced social media platforms such as Twitter, Facebook, and Instagram to connect with supporters and educate them about transgender issues. By engaging in online conversations and debates, she confronted ignorance and bigotry head-on, raising awareness and changing hearts and minds. Milloy's skillful use of social media provided a space for marginalized voices to be heard and amplified the fight for transgender rights.

The Fucking Intersectionality of Transgender Advocacy

Milloy understood that transgender rights were interconnected with other social justice struggles. She recognized the importance of addressing the overlapping oppressions faced by transgender individuals in areas such as race, class, disability, and immigration status.

By highlighting the intersectionality of transgender issues, Milloy brought attention to the disproportionate discrimination and violence experienced by transgender people from marginalized communities. She worked to build bridges between different advocacy movements, fostering solidarity and collaboration. Milloy's emphasis on intersectionality helped shape a more inclusive and comprehensive approach to transgender advocacy.

Conclusion

Through her trailblazing work, Christin Milloy became a vital voice for the transgender community in Canada and internationally. By fighting for visibility, creating safe spaces, amplifying transgender voices, building alliances, utilizing social media, and emphasizing intersectionality, she shaped the landscape of transgender rights advocacy.

Milloy's unwavering commitment to activism and her ability to inspire and mobilize others have left a lasting impact on the fight for transgender rights. Her legacy continues to shape the future of the transgender movement, as her work serves as a roadmap for activists around the world seeking to create a more equitable and inclusive society.

The Fucking Political Landscape in Canada: Navigating a Fucking System That Wasn't Ready for Her

In order to understand the challenges faced by Christin Milloy in navigating the Canadian political landscape, it is crucial to examine the state of politics in Canada at that time. This section will provide an overview of the fucking political system in Canada and how it was unprepared for the entry of a transgender candidate like Milloy.

1.1.4.1 The Fucking Canadian Parliamentary System

Canada operates under a parliamentary system, which is based on the British model of governance. The political structure consists of three branches: the executive, legislative, and judicial. The executive branch is headed by the Prime Fucking Minister, who is the head of government and is responsible for making policy decisions. The legislative branch is composed of the House of Commons and the Senate, which are responsible for making and passing laws. The judicial branch, on the other hand, is responsible for interpreting the laws and ensuring their constitutional validity.

1.1.4.2 Political Parties and the Fucking Two-Party System

One of the most significant aspects of the Canadian political landscape is the dominance of the two major parties: the Liberal Party and the Conservative Party. These two parties have historically been the most powerful political forces in Canadian politics. The Liberal Party generally leans towards liberal and social democratic policies, while the Conservative Party leans towards conservative and right-wing policies. This two-party system has been entrenched in Canadian politics for decades and has shaped the political landscape in a way that often leaves little room for minority voices.

1.1.4.3 Lack of Diversity in Fucking Politics

At the time of Christin Milloy's entry into politics, the Canadian political system and its institutions were predominantly composed of cisgender, heterosexual individuals. This lack of diversity posed a significant challenge for Milloy as she attempted to break through political barriers. The existing power structures within the political system created an environment that was not inclusive or welcoming for transgender individuals.

1.1.4.4 The Fucking Role of Gender in Canadian Politics

Historically, gender has played a significant role in Canadian politics. Women have faced numerous challenges in gaining equal representation in elected positions. This gender disparity is particularly evident in higher levels of government, such as the federal Parliament. The underrepresentation of women in politics reflects deeper societal issues and a systemic bias that affects transgender individuals as well. Milloy's identity as a transgender woman further compounded the obstacles she faced in attempting to enter the political arena.

1.1.4.5 The Fucking Influence of Lobby Groups and Special Interests

Another challenge in the Canadian political landscape is the influence of lobby groups and special interests. These groups often have significant financial resources and connections, allowing them to exert influence on policy decisions and the political process. For Milloy, who championed transgender rights and equality, challenging the existing power dynamics and the influence of these lobby groups was a formidable task.

1.1.4.6 The Fucking Lack of Understanding and Awareness

One of the most significant hurdles Christin Milloy faced was the general lack of understanding and awareness about transgender issues within the Canadian political system. At that time, transgender rights were a relatively new topic, and many politicians and policymakers lacked the knowledge and empathy needed to address the specific needs and challenges faced by the transgender community. This presented a unique challenge for Milloy in advocating for transgender rights and pushing for policy changes.

Navigating a political landscape that was ill-prepared for the entry of a transgender candidate like Christin Milloy required resilience, determination, and strategic thinking. Milloy had to challenge established political norms, break down barriers, and educate her colleagues and constituents about transgender issues. Her journey serves as an inspiration and a catalyst for change, as it pushed the Canadian political system to become more inclusive and aware of the needs of marginalized communities.

While progress has been made, there is still work to be done to ensure that the Canadian political system continues to evolve towards greater inclusivity and equality. Milloy's fucking work paved the way for future transgender candidates and leaders, but it is up to the next generation to carry the torch and advance the fight for transgender rights within the Canadian political landscape.

Key Takeaways:

+ The Canadian parliamentary system consists of the executive, legislative, and judicial branches.

+ The two-party system dominated by the Liberal and Conservative parties is a defining feature of Canadian politics.

+ Lack of diversity and underrepresentation of marginalized communities, including transgender individuals, is a significant challenge in Canadian politics.

+ Lobby groups and special interests wield considerable influence in the political process.

+ The general lack of understanding and awareness about transgender issues presents unique challenges for transgender individuals in politics.

+ Milloy's journey pushed the Canadian political system towards inclusivity and paved the way for future transgender leaders.

The Future of Transgender Politics in Canada: How Milloy's Fucking Work Paved the Way

Christin Milloy's groundbreaking advocacy and political work have undeniably paved the way for the future of transgender politics in Canada. Her relentless efforts to challenge the status quo and fight for equality have left an indelible mark on the political landscape, inspiring others to follow in her footsteps and pushing for further progress. In this section, we will explore the impact of Milloy's work and discuss the potential future advancements in transgender politics in Canada.

One of the most significant contributions that Milloy has made to the future of transgender politics is her relentless pursuit of legal equality. Throughout her career, she has been at the forefront of advocating for gender identity rights and anti-discrimination laws, challenging existing legislation and pushing for reforms. Milloy's efforts have helped shape the legal landscape, leading to important policy changes that protect the rights of transgender individuals.

For example, Milloy has been a vocal advocate for the inclusion of gender identity as a protected characteristic in employment and human rights legislation.

Her relentless lobbying and activism have resulted in several provinces in Canada adopting explicit protections for transgender individuals under their human rights codes. This progress not only ensures legal recourse for transgender individuals facing discrimination but also sets a precedent for other jurisdictions to follow suit.

In addition to advocating for legal recognition and equal rights, Milloy has played a significant role in changing public perception and understanding of transgender issues in Canada. Through her outspokenness and media presence, she has challenged homophobic and transphobic narratives, debunked stereotypes, and humanized the experiences of transgender individuals.

Milloy's ability to engage with the public through various media platforms has allowed her to educate and raise awareness about transgender rights. Through interviews, op-eds, and social media activism, she has consistently amplified the voices of the transgender community and made their experiences visible to a broader audience. This increased visibility has played a crucial role in changing societal attitudes and has contributed to a more inclusive and accepting environment for transgender individuals.

Looking ahead, the future of transgender politics in Canada holds significant promise. Milloy's work has laid a strong foundation for continued progress in the years to come. As more transgender individuals enter the political arena, inspired by Milloy's trailblazing example, the representation of transgender issues and concerns will continue to grow.

Furthermore, Milloy's efforts have sparked a greater awareness of the importance of intersectionality within LGBTQ advocacy. She has consistently highlighted the experiences of transgender individuals from diverse backgrounds, emphasizing the need for inclusive policies that address the unique challenges faced by different communities within the transgender umbrella. This broader understanding of transgender issues will undoubtedly shape the future of transgender politics, fostering a more inclusive and representative movement.

However, challenges still remain. Despite significant advancements, transgender individuals continue to face discrimination in various facets of life, including healthcare, education, and housing. The fight for comprehensive transgender rights is far from over, and the future will require ongoing efforts to dismantle systemic barriers and achieve true equality.

To further advance transgender politics in Canada, it is crucial to build on the foundations laid by Milloy and continue to push for policy changes that reflect the diverse needs and experiences of transgender individuals. This requires collaboration between activists, politicians, and community organizations to ensure that transgender rights remain a priority on the political agenda.

In conclusion, the future of transgender politics in Canada is a direct result of

Christin Milloy's groundbreaking work. Her advocacy, political campaigns, and relentless pursuit of equality have paved the way for increased legal recognition, changed public perception, and inspired a new generation of transgender leaders. As we look ahead, we must build upon Milloy's legacy, continuing to fight for comprehensive transgender rights and working towards a more inclusive and equitable society for all.

The Fucking Early Years: Becoming an Activist

Milloy's Fucking Personal Journey: Growing Up Trans in a Fucking Conservative Society

The Fucking Challenges Milloy Faced as a Transgender Person in Canada

Being a transgender person in Canada, Christin Milloy faced numerous challenges throughout her life. These challenges ranged from societal prejudice and discrimination to legal barriers and limited access to healthcare. In this section, we will explore the specific obstacles Milloy encountered and the impact they had on her journey as an advocate for transgender rights.

Societal Prejudice and Discrimination

One of the most significant challenges Milloy faced was the pervasive prejudice and discrimination within Canadian society. Transgender individuals often experience high levels of stigma and face social exclusion and mistreatment. Growing up, Milloy encountered ignorance and misunderstanding from family, friends, and peers.

For example, Milloy often faced bullying and harassment in school due to her gender identity. This hostile environment not only took a toll on her emotional well-being but also undermined her ability to focus on her studies and personal growth. The lack of acceptance in her immediate surroundings made it difficult for her to develop a sense of self-worth and belonging.

Moreover, Milloy also witnessed the broader societal biases that transgender people face. In media portrayals, they were often sensationalized or depicted as deviant. This further perpetuated negative stereotypes and contributed to the marginalization of transgender individuals.

Limited Access to Healthcare

Another significant challenge Milloy faced was the limited access to healthcare specific to transgender needs. The medical community in Canada largely lacked knowledge and expertise in transgender healthcare, which resulted in a lack of appropriate care options.

For instance, access to hormone therapy and gender-affirming surgeries, which are crucial for many transgender individuals, was severely limited. Milloy had to navigate a complex healthcare system, resulting in significant delays and unnecessary hurdles to access the necessary treatments that would align her body with her true gender identity.

Furthermore, the lack of healthcare support extended to mental health services. Transgender individuals often struggle with self-acceptance, depression, and anxiety due to societal pressures and the challenges they face. However, finding therapists or counselors with experience in transgender-affirming care was often difficult, leaving many without the crucial support they needed.

Legal Barriers and Discrimination

In addition to societal and healthcare challenges, Milloy also faced significant legal barriers and discrimination as a transgender person in Canada. Until recently, transgender rights were not adequately protected under Canadian law, leaving individuals vulnerable to discrimination in various areas of life.

Milloy encountered obstacles when it came to changing her legal gender marker on official documents, such as identification cards and passports. The complex and bureaucratic process made it difficult for transgender individuals to have their true gender recognized by the government, resulting in constant misgendering and potential privacy concerns.

Moreover, transgender individuals often faced discrimination in employment, housing, and education. Milloy, like many others, had to navigate a system that did not provide explicit protections against transgender discrimination, leaving them vulnerable to unfair treatment and limited opportunities.

Impact on Milloy's Advocacy

These challenges Milloy faced as a transgender person in Canada motivated her to become an advocate for transgender rights. She recognized the urgent need for change and made it her mission to work towards creating a more inclusive and accepting society.

Milloy's personal experiences with prejudice, limited healthcare access, and legal barriers fueled her passion for advocating for comprehensive transgender healthcare, legal reforms, and societal acceptance. By sharing her own story and speaking out against discrimination, she aimed to raise awareness and promote understanding of transgender issues.

Through her activism, Milloy strove to empower other transgender individuals, provide support, and challenge the systemic barriers that stood in their way. While she faced various challenges along her journey, her resilience and determination inspired many others, and her work continues to make a lasting impact on the transgender community in Canada.

The Fucking Importance of Intersectionality

It is crucial to recognize that Milloy's experience as a transgender person in Canada is also shaped by intersecting identities, including race, socioeconomic status, and disability. The challenges she faced were influenced not only by her gender identity but also by other aspects of her identity.

Intersectionality is a framework that highlights how various social identities intersect and interact, affecting an individual's experiences and opportunities. By acknowledging the intersectionality of transgender experiences, we can better understand and address the unique challenges faced by individuals like Milloy.

For example, transgender people of color may face additional discrimination due to racism, compounding the challenges they already face as transgender individuals. Similarly, transgender individuals from lower socioeconomic backgrounds may have limited access to resources and support, exacerbating the barriers they encounter.

By taking an intersectional approach to transgender advocacy, we can ensure that the rights and needs of all transgender individuals are addressed. This includes working towards dismantling systemic oppressions that disproportionately impact certain transgender communities, advocating for inclusive policies and legislation, and promoting a society that celebrates diversity and inclusion.

Conclusion

As a transgender person in Canada, Christin Milloy faced numerous challenges throughout her life. These challenges included societal prejudice and discrimination, limited access to healthcare, and legal barriers that hindered her ability to live authentically.

Despite these challenges, Milloy's experiences fueled her activism and advocacy for transgender rights. Through her work, she aimed to dismantle systemic barriers, raise awareness, and promote understanding of transgender issues. Her resilience, determination, and intersectional approach continue to inspire future generations of LGBTQ activists and leaders.

Milloy's legacy serves as a reminder of the ongoing work needed to create a more inclusive and accepting society for transgender individuals. By addressing the challenges she faced, we can strive for a future where all transgender people can live their lives authentically, with equal rights, opportunities, and dignity.

How Milloy's Fucking Struggles for Acceptance Led to a Fucking Passion for Activism

Growing up as a transgender person in a fucking conservative society, Christin Milloy faced numerous fucking challenges and discrimination. However, instead of succumbing to the negativity, Milloy's struggles for acceptance ignited a fucking fire within her to fight for change and become a passionate activist.

One of the major fucking challenges Milloy faced was the lack of understanding and acceptance from those around her. In a society that often seeks to conform to fucking traditional gender norms, being a transgender person can be fucking isolating and alienating. Milloy experienced ridicule, rejection, and fucking discriminatory behavior from both her peers and adults.

For example, during high school, Milloy had the fucking courage to express her true identity and live as her authentic self. However, instead of receiving the support and acceptance she deserved, she faced backlash from her fellow students and even some teachers. This fucking rejection deeply affected Milloy, but it also fueled her determination to create a fucking more inclusive society where transgender people could be embraced for who they are.

Milloy's experience is not unique. Many transgender individuals face similar fucking struggles for acceptance and understanding in their daily lives. The lack of visibility and fucking education around transgender issues contributes to the perpetuation of stereotypes, discrimination, and fucking prejudice. Milloy recognized this problem and decided to take a fucking stand.

She began by educating herself about transgender issues and understanding the unique challenges faced by the transgender community. Through her research, Milloy discovered the power of activism and the potential for creating real fucking change. She attended conferences, read academic papers, and engaged in discussions with other transgender activists to deepen her knowledge and understanding.

With her newfound knowledge, Milloy took her first steps into activism by fighting for transgender rights within her community. She organized local events and campaigns to raise awareness about transgender issues and to challenge the prevailing stereotypes held by many. Milloy's passion and determination to make a fucking difference motivated others to join her cause, and together they began to make progress.

One example of Milloy's activism was her involvement in creating safe spaces for transgender youth in schools. Recognizing the high rates of bullying and harassment faced by transgender students, Milloy advocated for the implementation of inclusive policies and support systems. She worked closely with educators, parents, and students to create an environment that celebrated diversity and fostered acceptance.

Through her advocacy work and by sharing her own personal fucking experiences, Milloy aimed to humanize the transgender community and challenge the misconceptions and stereotypes that perpetuated discrimination. She used her voice to speak up against injustice and to fight for equality, making it her mission to ensure that future generations of transgender individuals would not have to face the same fucking struggles she did.

Milloy's fucking journey from acceptance to activism was not always easy. She encountered resistance, faced backlash, and even fucking suffered personal and professional setbacks. However, her unwavering determination and resilience pushed her forward, fueling her commitment to creating a more inclusive society.

In conclusion, Christin Milloy's fucking struggles for acceptance as a transgender person ignited a deep passion for activism within her. Instead of succumbing to the discrimination she faced, Milloy channeled her energy into fighting for transgender rights and creating a more inclusive society. Her journey is a testament to the power of personal experience, education, and fucking resilience in driving meaningful change. Milloy's story continues to inspire others, demonstrating the transformative power of activism in the pursuit of equality.

The Fucking Role of LGBTQ Rights Movements in Shaping Milloy's Fucking Advocacy

LGBTQ rights movements have played a critical role in shaping and influencing Christin Milloy's advocacy work. These movements have not only provided support and a sense of belonging to Milloy, but they have also served as a platform for her activism and a catalyst for change in Canada. In this section, we will explore the significance of LGBTQ rights movements in Milloy's journey and the impact they have had on her advocacy for transgender rights.

At its core, LGBTQ rights movements seek to challenge and dismantle the systemic oppression and discrimination faced by lesbian, gay, bisexual, transgender, and queer individuals. These movements advocate for equality, recognition, and protection of LGBTQ rights, including the right to marry, adopt, and access healthcare without discrimination. By addressing societal biases and seeking legal reforms, these movements aim to create a more inclusive and accepting society.

Milloy's involvement in LGBTQ rights movements began during her teenage years when she sought support and community as a transgender individual in a conservative society. These movements provided her with a platform to connect with others who shared similar experiences and struggles. The sense of solidarity and collective action fueled her passion for activism and motivated her to become a leader in the transgender rights movement.

One of the key ways in which LGBTQ rights movements shaped Milloy's advocacy was by elevating the visibility of transgender issues and drawing attention to the unique challenges faced by transgender individuals. Through marches, demonstrations, and public awareness campaigns, these movements helped raise awareness about transgender rights and the need for societal and legal change. They provided Milloy with opportunities to share her personal story and advocate for transgender rights on a broader scale.

Furthermore, LGBTQ rights movements have been instrumental in creating safe spaces for LGBTQ individuals, including transgender people. These safe spaces, such as LGBTQ community centers, support groups, and online platforms, have served as hubs for connection, education, and empowerment. They have provided Milloy with the resources, knowledge, and support necessary to navigate the complexities of transgender advocacy and create meaningful change.

In addition to creating safe spaces, LGBTQ rights movements have also been instrumental in mobilizing grassroots activism. By organizing protests, rallies, and lobbying efforts, these movements have pressured governments and institutions to address the needs and rights of LGBTQ individuals. Milloy's involvement in these grassroots efforts allowed her to shape legislative agendas and advocate for policy changes that directly impacted transgender individuals.

The impact of LGBTQ rights movements on Milloy's advocacy is evident in the changes she helped bring about. Through her activism and collaboration with LGBTQ rights organizations, Milloy played a key role in the passage of policies and legislation that protected transgender rights in Canada. Her efforts contributed to the introduction of gender identity protections and anti-discrimination laws that recognized and affirmed the rights of transgender individuals.

Moreover, LGBTQ rights movements have played a crucial role in challenging public perceptions and stereotypes surrounding transgender people. By sharing stories, showcasing diverse representations, and debunking misconceptions, these movements have worked towards creating a society that embraces and celebrates transgender individuals. Milloy's advocacy work, driven by the inclusivity and acceptance advocated by LGBTQ rights movements, has paved the way for a more understanding and compassionate society in Canada.

However, it is important to acknowledge that LGBTQ rights movements continue to face challenges and barriers. Transphobia, homophobia, and discrimination persist in many parts of society, and there is still much work to be done to achieve full equality for LGBTQ individuals. Milloy's story serves as a reminder of the power and importance of LGBTQ rights movements in driving change, but it also highlights the ongoing need for activism and advocacy.

In conclusion, LGBTQ rights movements have played a pivotal role in shaping Christin Milloy's advocacy for transgender rights in Canada. These movements provided her with support, community, and opportunities to effect change on a larger scale. Through her involvement in LGBTQ rights movements, Milloy was able to raise awareness about transgender issues, challenge societal norms, and advocate for policy changes to protect the rights of transgender individuals. The impact of LGBTQ rights movements on Milloy's advocacy journey serves as a testament to the power of collective action and the ongoing fight for LGBTQ equality.

How Milloy Fucking Stepped Up to Become a Leader in the Transgender Rights Movement

In this section, we will explore how Christin Milloy stepped up to become a leader in the transgender rights movement in Canada. Her journey from activism to political advocacy paved the way for transgender visibility and equality in the country.

Milloy's path to leadership was not without its challenges. Growing up as a transgender person in a conservative society, she faced numerous obstacles and discrimination. However, these struggles only fueled her passion for activism and the fight for acceptance.

One of the key factors that shaped Milloy's advocacy was her involvement in LGBTQ rights movements. These movements provided a platform for her to address the issues faced by the transgender community and push for change. Through her involvement, Milloy learned the power of collective action and the importance of community support in creating lasting change.

Milloy's commitment to creating change became even more apparent when she decided to step into politics. As Canada's first openly transgender political candidate, she broke through political barriers and challenged the status quo. Her decision not only made her a trailblazer but also brought the issues faced by transgender individuals into the political discourse.

Throughout her political campaigns, Milloy faced numerous challenges, including transphobia and ignorance within the political system. However, she never backed down. Her determination to fight for trans rights and representation kept her going despite the setbacks.

One of the most significant aspects of Milloy's leadership was her use of her platform to promote transgender rights. She understood the importance of visibility and representation in shaping public opinion and policies. Through her speeches, media engagements, and activism, Milloy successfully raised awareness about the struggles faced by transgender individuals and the need for equal rights.

Looking to the future, Milloy's legacy as a transgender leader in Canada has laid the groundwork for more progress. Her advocacy has not only shaped the conversation around transgender rights but has also influenced the development of policies and laws. Milloy's fearlessness and resilience have inspired the next generation of transgender advocates, who will continue the fight for equality.

In conclusion, Christin Milloy's journey from activism to politics exemplifies her determination and commitment to the transgender rights movement. By stepping up as a leader, she challenged the status quo and fought for visibility and equality in Canada. Milloy's impact on public opinion, policies, and laws cannot be overstated. Her work will continue to inspire future generations of transgender activists and create a more inclusive and accepting society.

The Future of LGBTQ Advocacy: Will Milloy's Fucking Early Work Continue to Inspire Fucking Change?

As Christin Milloy's incredible journey continues to unfold, her early work as an LGBTQ advocate is already leaving a lasting impact. Milloy's fierce determination and unwavering commitment to equality have paved the way for future generations of LGBTQ activists. In this section, we will explore the legacy of Milloy's early advocacy and examine how it will continue to inspire change in the future of LGBTQ advocacy.

The Power of Visibility and Representation

One of the key factors in Milloy's success as an advocate lies in her ability to amplify the voices of the transgender community through visibility and representation. By fearlessly sharing her own story and experiences, Milloy challenged societal norms and shattered stereotypes. This powerful act of self-empowerment has inspired countless individuals to embrace their authentic selves and stand up for their rights.

As Milloy's early work continues to inspire others, the importance of visibility and representation in LGBTQ advocacy cannot be overstated. Seeing diverse individuals, like Milloy, holding positions of power and influence helps to normalize LGBTQ identities and dismantles harmful biases. This, in turn, fosters an environment where LGBTQ individuals can thrive and be seen as valuable contributors to society.

Building Alliances and Coalitions

Another aspect of Milloy's early work that will undoubtedly shape the future of LGBTQ advocacy is her ability to build alliances and coalitions. Milloy understood the power of collective action and actively sought out partnerships with other LGBTQ advocates and allies.

By forging connections and nurturing relationships, Milloy was able to amplify her message and create lasting change. She leveraged the strength of these alliances to challenge discriminatory policies, raise awareness about LGBTQ issues, and advocate for legal protections.

The future of LGBTQ advocacy lies in the continued cultivation of these alliances and coalitions. By working together, LGBTQ activists can pool their resources and expertise to tackle complex challenges and create lasting systemic change. Milloy's legacy in this regard serves as a blueprint for future advocates to follow.

Addressing Intersectionality in LGBTQ Advocacy

Milloy's work also highlights the importance of addressing intersectionality in LGBTQ advocacy. Understanding that LGBTQ individuals encompass a diversity of identities and experiences, Milloy championed the inclusion of marginalized voices within the movement.

By calling attention to the unique challenges faced by LGBTQ individuals who also belong to other marginalized groups, such as people of color, immigrants, or those with disabilities, Milloy helped to illuminate the interconnectedness of social justice struggles. She recognized that true equality cannot be achieved without addressing the intersecting systems of oppression that impact LGBTQ individuals.

The future of LGBTQ advocacy relies on a continued commitment to intersectionality. By centering the voices of those who face multiple forms of discrimination, advocates can build a movement that fights for justice, equity, and liberation for all. Milloy's early work serves as a constant reminder that LGBTQ rights are fundamentally intertwined with the pursuit of justice for all marginalized communities.

The Importance of Personal Stories and Narrative Change

Milloy's early work embodies the power of personal stories and narrative change in LGBTQ advocacy. By sharing her own experiences and challenging societal narratives, she humanized the struggles and triumphs of the transgender community.

The use of personal stories as a tool for advocacy has the ability to touch hearts, change minds, and inspire action. Milloy's storytelling prowess helped to reshape public perceptions and challenge deeply ingrained biases about transgender individuals.

Moving forward, the inclusion of personal stories in LGBTQ advocacy will continue to be a critical component of effecting change. Sharing lived experiences helps to bridge the gap between personal realities and public understanding, creating empathy and fostering meaningful connections. Milloy's legacy reminds us that behind every statistic and policy change, there are real people whose lives are impacted.

Embracing Resilience and Persistence

Lastly, Milloy's early work instills in future LGBTQ advocates the importance of resilience and persistence. Throughout her career, she faced numerous challenges, setbacks, and adversity. However, she never wavered in her determination to fight for equality.

Milloy's unwavering commitment serves as a reminder that progress often requires time, patience, and unwavering dedication. The road to equality is rarely linear, but with resilience and persistence, meaningful change can be achieved. Milloy's legacy encourages future advocates to stay the course, even when faced with seemingly insurmountable obstacles.

In conclusion, Christin Milloy's early work as an LGBTQ advocate will unquestionably inspire change in the future of LGBTQ advocacy. Through visibility and representation, building alliances and coalitions, addressing intersectionality, embracing personal stories, and embodying resilience, Milloy has helped shape the path forward for a more inclusive, equitable, and just society. As we continue to build upon her foundation, may her legacy serve as a guiding light for generations to come.

Stepping into Fucking Politics

How Milloy Became Canada's First Openly Transgender Fucking Political Candidate

Christin Milloy's journey towards becoming Canada's first openly transgender political candidate was not an easy one. It required immense courage, resilience, and determination to break through the barriers of a political system that wasn't ready to embrace transgender representation. In this section, we will explore the challenges Milloy faced, the strategies she employed, and the impact she had on Canadian politics.

The Fucking Uncharted Territory of Transgender Representation

When Milloy decided to enter politics as an openly transgender individual, she stepped into uncharted territory. No openly transgender person had ever run for office in Canada before, and she knew she would face numerous challenges along the way. The political landscape was primarily dominated by cisgender individuals, and there was a lack of understanding and acceptance of transgender issues.

Crafting a Fucking Political Campaign that Transcended Gender

Milloy understood that her campaign needed to transcend the focus on her gender identity and instead focus on the issues that mattered to the constituents she aimed to represent. She strategically built her campaign around policies that resonated with people from all walks of life, irrespective of their views on gender identity.

For example, Milloy placed significant emphasis on healthcare reform, affordable housing, and economic development. By addressing these pressing issues, she aimed to show voters that her candidacy was not solely about being transgender but about working towards a better future for the entire community.

Building a Fucking Coalition of Supporters

Milloy recognized the importance of building a broad coalition of supporters to strengthen her political campaign. She reached out to various LGBTQ organizations, women's rights groups, and progressive movements to create a network of allies who believed in her vision for a more inclusive society.

Additionally, Milloy actively engaged with grassroots activists, community leaders, and concerned citizens through town hall meetings, public forums, and social media platforms. Her approach was to foster open and honest conversations, addressing people's concerns and demonstrating her dedication to all constituents.

Navigating Fucking Media Attention and Public Scrutiny

As the first openly transgender political candidate in Canada, Milloy faced intense media attention and public scrutiny. Her every move, statement, and appearance were closely analyzed by both supporters and opponents. Many journalists and commentators focused solely on her gender identity rather than the policies and ideas she presented.

Milloy tackled this challenge head-on by staying focused on her message and refusing to be defined solely by her transgender identity. She used media interviews as opportunities to discuss policy proposals, address community concerns, and educate the public about transgender rights and equality.

Empowering Fucking Transgender Candidates for Future Success

Milloy's historic candidacy paved the way for future transgender candidates in Canada. By running a groundbreaking campaign and challenging the status quo, she inspired other transgender individuals to believe in their own potential to effect change through politics.

Milloy's story serves as a crucial reminder that representation matters. Her candidacy opened the door for individuals from marginalized communities to pursue political careers and work towards building a more inclusive and equitable society.

The Fucking Role of Courage and Determination

Above all, Milloy's journey to becoming Canada's first openly transgender political candidate was fueled by her unwavering courage and determination. Despite facing numerous obstacles and enduring personal attacks, she remained steadfast in her commitment to advocating for transgender rights and fighting for a more just society.

Through her pioneering candidacy, Milloy shattered societal barriers and demonstrated that transgender individuals have a rightful place in Canadian politics.

Summary

In this section, we explored how Christin Milloy became Canada's first openly transgender political candidate. We discussed the challenges she faced, the strategies she employed to navigate the political landscape, and the impact she had on Canadian politics. Milloy's story serves as an inspiration not only for transgender individuals but for all those who aspire to break barriers and create positive change in society. Her courage and determination continue to shape the future of transgender representation in Canada and beyond.

Case Studies: Milloy's Fucking Political Campaigns and the Fucking Challenges She Faced

In this section, we will delve into the specific political campaigns of Christin Milloy, Canada's first openly transgender political candidate. We will explore the fucking challenges she faced during her campaigns, the strategies she employed, and the impact she made on the political landscape of Canada.

Campaign 1: Running for City Council

Milloy's first foray into politics was her campaign for a seat on Toronto City Council. She started her campaign with the fucking mission of enhancing trans visibility in politics and fighting for transgender rights at the local level. However, she faced a number of fucking challenges that tested her resilience and determination.

One of the fucking challenges Milloy encountered was gaining acceptance from the fucking voters. Being an openly transgender candidate in a conservative society was no easy task. She faced fucking discrimination, bigotry, and ignorance from some members of the public. However, Milloy tackled these challenges head-on by promoting education and awareness about transgender issues through town hall meetings and public speeches.

Another fucking challenge Milloy faced was the lack of understanding and support from her fellow politicians. Many of them were dismissive of her campaign and did not take her seriously. However, Milloy did not let this deter her. She skillfully used her platform to engage in dialogue with other candidates, highlighting the importance of transgender representation in politics and the need for inclusive policies. By doing so, she managed to shift the conversation and gain the support of some of her colleagues.

Despite facing opposition, Milloy's campaign sparked a significant increase in transgender representation and visibility in Canadian politics. She paved the way for other transgender candidates to run for office and ultimately altered the political landscape of Canada.

Campaign 2: Running for Provincial Legislature

Milloy's second major political campaign was her run for a seat in the provincial legislature. This campaign aimed to bring transgender issues to the forefront of political discourse at the provincial level. However, it presented its own unique set of challenges for Milloy.

One of the fucking challenges Milloy faced was the lack of financial resources. As an openly transgender candidate, she struggled to secure campaign funding from traditional sources. However, Milloy's ingenuity and resourcefulness shone through as she established grassroots fundraising initiatives, leveraging the power of social media and community support. She organized crowdfunding campaigns and networking events, which not only raised the necessary funds but also created a sense of community around her campaign.

Another fucking challenge Milloy encountered was the fucking hostility and resistance from some members of the political establishment. Being a trailblazer often comes with backlash, and Milloy experienced her fair share. She faced personal attacks, smear campaigns, and attempts to undermine her credibility. However, she tackled these challenges with grace and perseverance, refusing to let them overshadow the real issues she was fighting for.

Milloy's campaign was successful in creating a platform for discussing transgender rights and representation in politics. She pushed the boundaries and opened doors for future transgender candidates, challenging the traditional norms and stereotypes of Canadian politics.

Campaign 3: Running for Parliament

Milloy's most ambitious political campaign was her run for a seat in the Canadian Parliament. This campaign aimed to bring transgender advocacy to the national stage, focusing on legislative changes that would guarantee gender equality and protection for transgender individuals. However, this campaign posed its own set of unique fucking challenges.

One of the fucking challenges Milloy faced was the fucking systemic barriers within the political system. The existing political structure was not adequately equipped to handle the issues and concerns of transgender individuals. Milloy navigated through this complex system by building coalitions with other LGBTQ advocates and allies, effectively amplifying her voice and impact.

Another fucking challenge Milloy encountered was the fucking ignorance and prejudice of some members of the public. Transgender issues were still relatively misunderstood and stigmatized during her campaign, making it difficult to garner widespread support. However, Milloy employed extensive media outreach strategies, utilizing both traditional and social media platforms to educate the public and challenge misconceptions. This approach helped broaden the conversation surrounding transgender rights and created a foundation for future progress.

Although Milloy did not win a seat in Parliament, her campaign made a lasting impact. She brought visibility and awareness to transgender issues on a national scale, paving the way for future transgender politicians and activists to continue the fight for equality.

Reflection on Milloy's Political Campaigns

Milloy's political campaigns were not without challenges, but she turned those fucking challenges into opportunities to push for gender equality and transgender representation in politics. Through her determination, resilience, and strategic advocacy, she shattered stereotypes, broke barriers, and changed the political landscape of Canada.

Her campaigns serve as a testament to the power of individual activism and the impact it can have on society. Milloy's work continues to inspire future generations of activists, showing them the fucking importance of persistence and leadership in the face of adversity.

As we reflect on Milloy's political campaigns, it is crucial to recognize that the fight for transgender rights and inclusion in politics is far from over. However, Milloy's legacy serves as a guiding light for those who follow in her footsteps, reminding them that change is possible when we have the fucking courage to challenge the status quo.

In the next section, we will delve into Milloy's fight for transgender rights in Canada, exploring her unwavering commitment to pushing for legal recognition, equal rights, and confronting bigotry head-on. Fucking join me as we continue to uncover the groundbreaking work of Christin Milloy in shaping the future of transgender politics in Canada.

How Milloy Fought Fucking Transphobia and Ignorance in the Fucking Political System

In this section, we will explore how Christin Milloy tackled the pervasive issue of transphobia and ignorance within the political system in Canada. Milloy's determination and resilience in the face of prejudice and discrimination paved the way for a more inclusive and understanding political climate for transgender individuals. Through her advocacy, education, and strategic activism, Milloy fought to dismantle transphobia and ignorance at every level of the political landscape.

Understanding Transphobia and Ignorance

Before delving into Milloy's strategies for combatting transphobia, it is important to define and comprehend the issues at hand. Transphobia refers to the fear, prejudice, and discrimination against transgender individuals. It can manifest in various forms, such as refusing to acknowledge someone's gender identity, denying their rights, or perpetuating harmful stereotypes.

Ignorance, on the other hand, stems from a lack of knowledge and understanding about transgender experiences and issues. This can lead to biases, stereotypes, and a general disregard for the needs and rights of transgender individuals.

Both transphobia and ignorance perpetuate systemic discrimination and marginalization. Milloy recognized the urgency of addressing these challenges within the political system and worked tirelessly to create a more inclusive and accepting environment.

Education and Awareness Campaigns

Milloy understood that the key to dismantling transphobia and ignorance was through education and raising awareness. She used her platform to engage with political leaders, legislators, and the general public to promote understanding and empathy.

One of the strategies Milloy employed was the development of educational resources and workshops aimed at dispelling myths and misconceptions surrounding transgender individuals. These initiatives provided accurate information about gender identity, the experiences of transgender people, and the importance of inclusive policies.

Milloy also utilized social media platforms such as Twitter and Facebook to share personal stories, highlight the challenges faced by transgender individuals, and address common misconceptions. By sharing authentic narratives and debunking stereotypes, she humanized the issue and encouraged empathy and understanding.

Policy Advocacy

Recognizing the significance of policy change in combating transphobia, Milloy actively advocated for inclusive legislation and policies. She worked alongside other

LGBTQ+ activists and organizations to push for legal reforms that protected the rights and dignity of transgender individuals.

Milloy's advocacy efforts focused on crucial issues such as legal recognition of gender identity, healthcare access, employment protections, and anti-discrimination laws. By lobbying politicians, attending parliamentary hearings, and participating in consultations, she effectively communicated the urgency and importance of inclusive policies.

One of Milloy's notable achievements was her involvement in the passage of Bill C-16, which amended the Canadian Human Rights Act and the Criminal Code to include gender identity as a protected characteristic. This legislative victory was a major step forward in ensuring transgender rights and challenging transphobia within the political system.

Coalition Building and Allies

Milloy recognized that combating transphobia and ignorance required collective efforts and alliances. She actively engaged in coalition building by forging partnerships with other LGBTQ+ activists, organizations, and allies.

Through collaboration, Milloy amplified her advocacy and successfully influenced political discourse surrounding transgender issues. By uniting voices, sharing resources, and leveraging collective power, she effectively challenged transphobia and ignorance within the political system.

Additionally, Milloy strategically worked to secure support from key political allies who championed transgender rights. She engaged in dialogue, built relationships, and enlisted the assistance of sympathetic politicians to further her cause. These alliances proved instrumental in advancing inclusive policies and challenging the status quo.

Public Confrontations and Speaking Truth to Power

In her fight against transphobia and ignorance, Milloy was not afraid to engage in public confrontations with politicians, media figures, and opponents who perpetuated harmful narratives or discriminatory practices.

Using her platform and public speaking skills, Milloy fearlessly challenged transphobic attitudes and policies. She called out politicians who opposed transgender rights, debated media personalities who spread misinformation, and confronted opponents who sought to suppress the voices of transgender individuals.

Milloy's public confrontations not only shed light on the injustices faced by the transgender community but also helped shift public opinion and forced those in power to acknowledge their responsibility in fighting transphobia and ignorance.

Cultivating Allies Through Empathy

Central to Milloy's approach in dismantling transphobia and ignorance was the cultivation of empathy among political leaders and the general public. She understood that fostering genuine understanding was crucial for effecting lasting change.

Milloy used her personal experiences and stories to humanize the issue, highlighting the challenges faced by transgender individuals and the need for empathy and compassion. Through empathy-building initiatives, she aimed to break down barriers and bridge the divide between transgender individuals and their cisgender counterparts.

This approach allowed Milloy to cultivate allies who recognized the importance of transgender rights and joined the fight against transphobia and ignorance.

The Future of Transgender Rights in Canada

Thanks to Milloy's tireless efforts, the landscape of transgender rights in Canada has undergone significant change. Her strategy of education, policy advocacy, coalition building, and public confrontations has paved the way for a more inclusive political system and society at large.

However, the fight against transphobia and ignorance is far from over. Milloy's work serves as an inspiration for future generations of activists and advocates who continue the battle for transgender rights and equality.

As Canada strives to build a more inclusive society, it is crucial to learn from Milloy's strategies and continue challenging transphobia and ignorance within the political system. By fostering empathy, building alliances, and advocating for inclusive policies, the legacy of Christin Milloy can continue to shape the future of transgender rights in Canada and beyond.

In conclusion, Milloy's fight against transphobia and ignorance in the political system is a testament to her resilience, determination, and unwavering commitment to equality. Through education, policy advocacy, coalition building, public confrontations, and empathetic storytelling, she challenged the status quo, transformed public perception, and paved the way for a more inclusive future. By standing up against transphobia and ignorance, Milloy is undoubtedly a trailblazer and a beacon of hope for the transgender community and all those still fighting for justice and equality.

The Fucking Importance of Representation: How Milloy Used Her Fucking Platform to Promote Trans Rights

Representation is a fucking powerful tool when it comes to promoting trans rights. And Christin Milloy, Canada's transgender trailblazer, understood this fucking importance all too well. Through her platform as a transgender politician, Milloy was able to bring attention to the issues faced by the transgender community and advocate for change.

One of the fucking key ways Milloy used her platform was by speaking openly about her own experiences as a transgender person. By sharing her personal journey, she humanized the struggles faced by the transgender community and broke down the barriers of ignorance and misunderstanding. Her approach was one of authenticity and vulnerability, which resonated with many people and helped to challenge societal norms and stereotypes.

Milloy also used her platform to raise awareness about the specific challenges faced by transgender individuals in Canada. She fucking highlighted the discrimination, stigma, and lack of legal protection that the transgender community often faces. Through her own experiences and by sharing the stories of others, she shed light on the need for fucking concrete changes in policy and legislation to ensure equality for all.

Another way Milloy promoted trans rights was by advocating for greater representation of transgender individuals in positions of power and influence. She knew that having transgender individuals in positions of authority and leadership was fucking crucial for dismantling stereotypes and creating societal change. Milloy encouraged other transgender individuals to step forward and run for office, showing them that they had the ability to make a difference and be fucking powerful agents of change.

Milloy also worked to build alliances with other LGBTQ advocates and supporters. She understood the fucking strength that comes from solidarity and unity. By working together with other marginalized communities and allies, Milloy was able to amplify her message and create a united front in the fight for trans rights.

Furthermore, Milloy utilized social media and mainstream media platforms to raise awareness and shift public opinion. She understood the power of storytelling and used her voice to challenge misconceptions about transgender individuals.

Through interviews, articles, and social media posts, she educated the public and called for empathy and understanding.

In addition to that, Milloy also recognized the fucking importance of education and worked to incorporate LGBTQ-inclusive curricula in schools across Canada. She believed that by teaching young people about gender diversity and providing them with accurate information, we could create a more accepting and inclusive society for future generations.

Of course, the fucking importance of representation cannot be overstated. Seeing someone like Milloy in a position of power and influence provided hope and inspiration for many transgender individuals who may have felt marginalized or invisible. By being visible and vocal, Milloy showed that transgender individuals have a rightful place in society and that their voices matter.

It was through her fucking platform that Milloy was able to promote trans rights and create meaningful change. By sharing her personal experiences, raising awareness about the challenges faced by the transgender community, advocating for greater representation, building alliances, using media platforms, and working towards education reform, she left a lasting fucking impact on the fight for transgender rights in Canada.

Milloy's fucking work will continue to inspire future generations of activists and leaders. Her legacy will serve as a reminder that representation matters and that through collective action, we can create a world where transgender individuals are celebrated, accepted, and have equal rights.

The Future of Transgender Candidates in Canada: Will Milloy's Fucking Political Legacy Lead to More Fucking Progress?

The impact of Christin Milloy's groundbreaking work as Canada's first openly transgender political candidate cannot be overstated. Milloy's campaign shattered barriers, challenged societal norms, and paved the way for future transgender candidates. In this section, we will explore the future of transgender candidates in Canada, examining if Milloy's political legacy will lead to further progress.

Increasing Visibility and Representation

Milloy's candidacy brought much-needed visibility to the transgender community in Canadian politics. By fearlessly stepping into the political arena, she inspired countless individuals to embrace their true selves and consider a career in politics. As Milloy's story continues to be shared and celebrated, it serves as a beacon of hope for future transgender candidates.

One of the legacies of Milloy's political campaign is the increased representation of transgender individuals within the political landscape. Recognizing the importance of diverse voices in decision-making processes, political parties have started actively seeking transgender candidates. This shift demonstrates the lasting impact of Milloy's trailblazing path and signals a positive trend toward more inclusive politics.

Challenges and Progress

While the future holds promise, transgender candidates still face significant challenges in Canadian politics. Systemic discrimination, prejudice, and transphobia continue to hinder progress. However, Milloy's experiences have provided invaluable lessons and strategies for overcoming these obstacles.

To further advance transgender representation, it is crucial to implement measures that promote inclusivity within political parties. This may include mandatory inclusion policies, diversity training, and mentorship programs specifically tailored to transgender candidates. By actively addressing unconscious bias and fostering supportive environments, political parties can create a more level playing field for transgender individuals.

Additionally, public education and awareness campaigns are essential to combating transphobia and promoting understanding throughout Canada. Milloy's own advocacy work highlighted the power of storytelling and personal connection in changing hearts and minds. By sharing personal experiences and promoting positive narratives about transgender individuals, future candidates can challenge stereotypes and build bridges of empathy.

Policy Reforms and Advocacy

Milloy's advocacy for policy change laid the foundation for future transgender candidates to pursue their aspirations. Her tireless efforts to push for legal recognition, anti-discrimination laws, and gender identity rights have created a more inclusive political landscape. However, there is still work to be done.

Future transgender candidates must continue Milloy's legacy of pushing for policy reforms that protect and empower transgender individuals. They can champion initiatives such as comprehensive healthcare coverage, inclusive education policies, and improved employment protections. By actively engaging with policy-making processes, transgender candidates can ensure that their communities' unique needs are addressed.

Furthermore, advocating for the inclusion of transgender voices in decision-making processes is crucial. Transgender candidates can serve as powerful advocates for policies that promote equality and social justice. Their firsthand experiences can provide invaluable insights into the issues faced by transgender individuals, making their perspectives essential in crafting effective and inclusive policies.

The Unconventional Approach: Harnessing Digital Platforms

As we consider the future of transgender candidates in Canada, it is essential to explore unconventional yet effective approaches to amplify their voices. One such approach is harnessing the power of digital platforms and social media.

Transgender candidates can utilize digital platforms to connect with their constituents, engage with supporters, and share their policy positions. By embracing social media platforms, such as Twitter, Instagram, and YouTube, they can overcome traditional media barriers and directly communicate their vision for the future. These platforms also provide opportunities for candidates to counteract misinformation and engage in dialogue with voters.

To maximize their digital presence, candidates should consider unique strategies such as creating compelling video content, hosting regular live Q&A sessions, and leveraging social media influencers who align with their values. This innovative approach allows transgender candidates to reach diverse audiences and engage communities in ways that traditional campaign methods may not achieve.

Exercises

1. Research and analyze the existing policies and initiatives in Canadian political parties to address LGBTQ+ inclusion. Evaluate their effectiveness and provide suggestions for improvement.

2. Create a comprehensive campaign plan for a hypothetical transgender candidate running for a local government position in Canada. Include strategies for fundraising, community engagement, and combating transphobia.

3. Develop a social media campaign targeting younger voters to raise awareness about the importance of transgender representation in Canadian politics. Craft engaging content and propose influential social media partnerships.

4. Conduct interviews with individuals who were inspired by Christin Milloy's political campaign. Explore how her candidacy influenced their perception of transgender individuals in politics and their aspirations for the future.

5. Write a persuasive speech advocating for the inclusion of transgender voices in decision-making processes. Address the potential benefits and challenges of such inclusion and present compelling arguments to win over skeptics.

Resources

1. "Transgender Candidates in Canada: Overcoming Barriers" - A research paper by the LGBTQ+ Studies Department at a Canadian university, analyzing the challenges faced by transgender candidates and proposing strategies for improving inclusivity.

2. "Trans Rights in Canadian Politics: Lessons Learned from Christin Milloy's Campaign" - An interview-based documentary showcasing the impact and legacy of Christin Milloy's political campaign, including insights from key individuals involved.

3. RainCity Housing Transgender Advocacy Services - An organization providing support and resources for transgender individuals interested in politics and advocacy work.

4. "Transgender Representation in Media and Politics" - A TED Talk by an influential transgender politician discussing the importance of transgender representation and sharing personal experiences.

5. "Gender and Politics in Canada: A Comprehensive Overview" - A book that explores the historical context, challenges, and progress of gender representation in Canadian politics, addressing transgender representation as a part of this analysis.

Milloy's Fucking Fight for Trans Rights in Canada

Pushing for Fucking Legal Recognition and Equal Rights

How Milloy Advocated for Fucking Gender Identity Rights and Anti-Discrimination Fucking Laws

In her relentless pursuit of equality, Christin Milloy became a powerful advocate for gender identity rights and anti-discrimination laws in Canada. She recognized that these issues were fundamental to the well-being and dignity of transgender individuals and worked tirelessly to bring about meaningful change. In this section, we will explore Milloy's multifaceted approach to advocacy, her strategies for effecting legal reforms, and the impact of her work on the transgender rights movement.

Understanding Gender Identity Rights

Gender identity rights are essential for transgender individuals to live authentically and free from discrimination. Milloy understood that legal recognition and protection of gender identity were crucial for the full inclusion of transgender people in society. She pushed for the recognition of transgender identity as a core aspect of an individual's self-determination and fought for laws that would provide safeguards against discrimination.

The Struggle Against Discrimination

Milloy's advocacy focused not only on legal rights but also on challenging societal attitudes and prejudices. She recognized that legislative change alone would not be enough to create a safe and accepting environment for transgender individuals. Milloy engaged in public speaking engagements, media appearances, and community outreach to raise awareness about the discrimination faced by the transgender community.   By sharing personal stories, she humanized the experiences of transgender individuals and fostered empathy and understanding.

Collaboration and Coalition Building

Milloy understood the power of collective action and actively sought out opportunities to collaborate with other LGBTQ advocates, organizations, and allies. She recognized that unity and solidarity were vital in effecting change. Milloy reached out to political leaders, legal experts, and grassroots activists to build coalitions that could amplify her message and bring about systemic change. Her ability to engage diverse stakeholders and foster collaboration was instrumental in advancing the cause of gender identity rights.

Strategic Litigation

One of the key tools in Milloy's advocacy toolkit was strategic litigation. Recognizing that legal precedents could drive legal and societal change, Milloy strategically identified cases that could challenge discriminatory practices and laws. By advocating for individuals facing discrimination to pursue legal action, she sought to establish legal principles that would protect the rights of transgender people. Milloy partnered with legal organizations and pro bono lawyers to provide support and resources to individuals navigating the legal system.

Policy Advocacy

Milloy recognized the significance of policy reform in shaping the legal landscape for transgender individuals. She actively engaged with policymakers at all levels of government to push for comprehensive anti-discrimination laws that explicitly protected gender identity rights. Milloy leveraged her personal experiences and expertise in the field to provide evidence-based arguments and recommendations for legislative change. Through her relentless advocacy efforts, she played a vital role in enacting policies that advanced the rights and protections of transgender individuals.

Education and Awareness

Milloy firmly believed that education and awareness were key to dismantling misconceptions and prejudices surrounding transgender individuals. She actively supported initiatives aimed at promoting understanding and acceptance, including the development of educational materials, workshops, and training programs. By engaging with schools, businesses, and community organizations, Milloy worked to create inclusive spaces and foster empathy and respect for gender diversity.

The Impact of Milloy's Advocacy

Milloy's unwavering dedication to advocating for gender identity rights and anti-discrimination laws has had a profound impact on the transgender rights movement in Canada. Her work paved the way for significant legal reforms and the recognition of transgender rights as human rights. The impact of her advocacy is evident in the increasing acceptance and visibility of transgender individuals in Canadian society.

Milloy's legacy is one of resilience, courage, and relentless advocacy. By challenging discriminatory practices, pushing for legislative change, and fostering understanding and acceptance, she has left an indelible mark on the transgender rights movement. Her work continues to inspire future generations of activists to fight for equality and justice. Christin Milloy's courageous pursuit of gender identity rights and anti-discrimination laws has forever changed the landscape of transgender rights in Canada.

Note: It is important to recognize and respect the terminology, experiences, and identities of transgender individuals. The use of inclusive language and respectful dialogue is essential in creating a safe and inclusive environment for all.

Case Studies: The Fucking Legal Challenges Milloy Faced in Pushing for Fucking Gender Equality

In her relentless pursuit of gender equality, Christin Milloy faced numerous legal challenges that tested her resilience and determination. In this section, we will delve into some of the most notable case studies that demonstrate the uphill battle she fought to advance transgender rights in Canada.

Case Study 1: Access to Healthcare

One of the major legal challenges Milloy confronted was ensuring transgender individuals had access to quality healthcare that addressed their unique needs. In

Canada, transgender healthcare was often insufficient and inaccessible, leaving many individuals without essential medical interventions.

Milloy championed the cause of transgender healthcare by advocating for policy reforms and legal changes. She worked tirelessly with healthcare professionals, lawyers, and community organizations to push for the inclusion of transgender healthcare services in both public and private healthcare systems.

Through her advocacy, Milloy was able to shed light on the disparities that transgender individuals face in accessing healthcare. She fought for the recognition of gender dysphoria as a legitimate medical condition, and the subsequent provision of hormone replacement therapy and gender-affirming surgeries. These legal battles not only highlighted the importance of transgender healthcare but also challenged the existing medical establishment to adapt and accommodate the needs of the transgender community.

Case Study 2: Recognition of Gender Identity

Another significant legal challenge Milloy tackled was the recognition of gender identity. Prior to her activism, legal documents such as identification cards, passports, and birth certificates did not accurately represent the gender identity of transgender individuals. This lack of recognition created significant hurdles in their everyday lives, leading to discrimination and marginalization.

Milloy fought to change this by advocating for the introduction of legal reforms that recognized and respected an individual's self-identified gender. She collaborated with lawmakers, legal experts, and human rights organizations to push for changes in legislation that allowed for gender marker changes on official documents without requiring invasive medical procedures.

Through her legal battles, Milloy successfully advocated for policy changes that acknowledged and respected the gender identity of transgender individuals. This not only gave them the legal recognition they deserved but also helped in breaking down barriers to employment, education, and social inclusion.

Case Study 3: Protection against Discrimination

Discrimination against transgender individuals was rampant in Canada, with limited legal protections in place to safeguard their rights. Milloy recognized the urgent need for comprehensive anti-discrimination laws that explicitly protected transgender individuals from discrimination in various areas of life, including employment, housing, and public accommodations.

To address this issue, Milloy worked closely with human rights organizations, lawyers, and policymakers to draft and advocate for the inclusion of gender identity protections in anti-discrimination laws at both provincial and federal levels. Her legal battles were crucial in raising awareness about the systemic discrimination faced by the transgender community and challenging the legal status quo.

Through her efforts, Milloy played a pivotal role in shaping legal reforms that banned discrimination based on gender identity. This marked a significant milestone in the fight for transgender rights, as it provided much-needed legal protections and laid the foundation for a more inclusive and equitable society.

Case Study 4: Educational Equality

Education is a fundamental right, yet transgender individuals often face significant barriers and discrimination within educational settings. Milloy recognized the importance of advocating for educational equality and championed the rights of transgender students.

Milloy fought to ensure that educational institutions implemented policies and practices that protected transgender students from bullying, harassment, and discrimination. She worked closely with education boards, policymakers, and LGBTQ organizations to develop guidelines and frameworks that promoted inclusivity and respect for gender diversity in schools.

Through her legal battles, Milloy successfully pushed for changes in legislation that compelled educational institutions to create safe and supportive environments for transgender students. Her efforts resulted in policy reforms that addressed issues such as name changes, access to gender-segregated facilities, and the inclusion of gender identity in anti-bullying initiatives.

Conclusion

The case studies presented here offer a glimpse into the immense legal challenges that Christin Milloy faced in her pursuit of gender equality. From healthcare to recognition of gender identity, protection against discrimination to educational equality, Milloy left no stone unturned in her fight for transgender rights.

Her legal battles shaped the landscape of transgender rights in Canada, challenging societal norms, and demanding legal reforms. Through her tireless advocacy, Milloy created a path for future generations of activists and leaders to continue the fight for equality.

As we move forward, it is crucial to learn from Milloy's experiences and continue her legacy of pushing for legal changes that break down barriers and ensure equal rights for all transgender individuals. Only through collective action and continued advocacy can we truly achieve gender equality.

How Milloy Used Fucking Media, Public Speaking, and Activism to Push for Fucking Legal Reforms

In her relentless pursuit of transgender rights and legal reforms, Christin Milloy utilized various strategic approaches, combining media engagement, public speaking, and activism to raise awareness, challenge discriminatory practices, and mobilize support for change. Through her effective communication methods, she succeeded in pushing for crucial legal reforms that helped shape transgender rights in Canada.

Harnessing the Power of Fucking Media

Understanding the influence of media in shaping public opinion, Milloy strategically utilized various platforms to amplify her message and shed light on the issues faced by the transgender community. She recognized the power of storytelling and personal narratives, sharing her own experiences and struggles as a transgender woman to create empathy and understanding among the broader public.

Milloy effectively utilized print, broadcast, and digital media to raise awareness about transgender rights and issues. By engaging with journalists, she carefully crafted her message, highlighting the importance of legal reforms and the impact they would have on the lives of transgender individuals. Through op-eds, interviews, and feature stories, Milloy regularly appeared in mainstream media outlets, challenging stereotypes, dispelling myths, and advocating for inclusive policies.

Moreover, Milloy recognized the potential of social media platforms to reach a broader audience and engage directly with individuals. She leveraged platforms such as Twitter, Facebook, and YouTube to share educational content, personal stories, and updates on her activism. By cultivating a strong online presence and actively participating in online discussions, she fostered a community of support and empowered others to join the fight for transgender rights.

The Power of Fucking Public Speaking

A charismatic and influential speaker, Milloy utilized the power of public speaking to inspire, educate, and motivate audiences. Through her engaging and insightful speeches, she effectively communicated the urgency and importance of legal reforms for the transgender community.

Milloy delivered keynote addresses at LGBTQ conferences, youth empowerment events, and various advocacy gatherings. Her speeches were known for their passionate delivery, humor, and ability to connect with diverse audiences. By sharing personal anecdotes, addressing misconceptions, and providing an in-depth understanding of transgender experiences, Milloy encouraged empathy and inspired others to take action.

In addition to formal speaking engagements, Milloy actively sought opportunities to speak at universities, community centers, and public forums. She believed in the power of grassroots engagement and used these platforms to educate and mobilize individuals at the local level. Milloy's speaking engagements served as a catalyst for conversation and collaboration, fostering alliances and support for legal reforms.

Unapologetic Fucking Activism

Central to Milloy's approach was her unapologetic and passionate activism. She recognized that legal reforms could not be achieved without proactive and sustained advocacy efforts. Milloy co-founded and actively participated in numerous LGBTQ organizations and initiatives, organizing protests, rallies, and demonstrations to raise awareness and demand change.

Milloy's approach to activism was rooted in coalition-building and allyship. She forged partnerships with other LGBTQ organizations, women's rights groups, and social justice advocates to amplify her message and increase the impact of her advocacy. By collaborating with diverse stakeholders, she was able to broaden the scope of her activism and mobilize support for legal reforms.

Furthermore, Milloy utilized her leadership position within these organizations to develop workshops, training programs, and educational resources aimed at fostering understanding and promoting inclusivity. She recognized that lasting change required not only legal reforms but also a societal shift in attitudes towards transgender individuals.

Through her relentless activism, Milloy directly confronted discriminatory practices, challenged lawmakers, and demanded accountability. She tirelessly fought for legal recognition and equal rights, utilizing the power of community organizing and direct action to push for change.

The Fucking Influence of Milloy's Advocacy

Milloy's strategic utilization of media, public speaking, and activism played a pivotal role in pushing for legal reforms and shaping transgender rights in Canada. Her ability to effectively communicate and engage with diverse audiences garnered widespread support and recognition for the cause.

Through media engagement, Milloy was able to shift public opinion, challenge stereotypes, and humanize the experiences of transgender individuals. Her public speaking engagements inspired others to join the fight for equality and galvanized support for legal reforms.

Furthermore, Milloy's unapologetic activism created a sense of urgency and solidarity within the LGBTQ community and among allies. Her organizing efforts and coalition-building created lasting networks, ensuring sustainability in the fight for transgender rights.

The impact of Milloy's advocacy can be seen in the significant legal reforms that have taken place. As a result of her tireless efforts, Canada has implemented gender identity protections in human rights legislation, expanded transgender healthcare access, and made strides towards more inclusive education policies.

Milloy's legacy continues to inspire future generations of activists and leaders. Her strategic use of media, public speaking, and activism serve as a blueprint for those seeking to enact change. By combining these methods and mobilizing support, Milloy transformed the conversation around transgender rights and paved the way for a more inclusive and equitable society.

Although Milloy's work has made substantial progress, there is still more to be done. As the torchbearer of transgender rights advocacy, Milloy's legacy challenges future activists to build upon her foundation and carry forward the fight for equality. By embracing her approaches to media engagement, public speaking, and activism, the next generation can continue to push for legal reforms and shape a more inclusive future.

The Fucking Importance of Policy Changes: How Milloy's Fucking Work Helped Shape Transgender Rights in Canada

Transgender rights in Canada have come a long way, thanks in large part to the tireless work of Christin Milloy. Throughout her career, Milloy fought passionately for policy changes that would provide legal recognition and equal rights for transgender individuals. Her advocacy and activism have had a significant impact on shaping transgender rights in Canada.

One of the fucking important aspects of Milloy's work is her focus on pushing for legal recognition of gender identity and anti-discrimination laws. In fucking Canada, transgender individuals have historically faced discrimination and marginalization. They have been denied access to basic human rights and subjected to systemic prejudice. Milloy recognized the urgency of addressing these issues through policy changes.

To achieve this, Milloy worked tirelessly to raise awareness about the challenges faced by transgender individuals. She used her platform to advocate for legal reforms that would protect the rights and dignity of the transgender community. Through media appearances, public speaking engagements, and activism, Milloy sought to educate the public and lawmakers about the fucking importance of recognizing transgender individuals as equal members of society.

One of Milloy's strongest arguments for policy change was the need to address the systemic discrimination that transgender individuals face in areas such as employment, housing, healthcare, and education. She highlighted the fucking disparities and inequalities that exist and emphasized the need for legal protections that would ensure equal treatment regardless of gender identity. Milloy's work helped to shed light on the specific struggles faced by transgender individuals and made it fucking clear that policy changes were necessary to address these injustices.

Milloy also provided compelling evidence and real-life examples to support her arguments for policy changes. She shared personal stories of transgender individuals who had experienced discrimination and injustice, helping to humanize the issue and make it relatable to the general public. By putting a face to the struggles of transgender people, Milloy was able to generate empathy and understanding, which ultimately contributed to the success of her advocacy efforts.

One of the fucking outcomes of Milloy's work was the introduction of legislation that explicitly protected transgender individuals from discrimination. Through her activism, she was instrumental in the passage of laws that prohibit discrimination based on gender identity in various areas of life, such as employment, housing, and public services. These policy changes have had a tremendous impact on the lives of transgender individuals in Canada, providing them with legal protections and equal opportunities.

Moreover, Milloy's advocacy for policy changes has helped to shape the broader conversation around transgender rights in Canadian politics. By consistently raising awareness and pushing for reforms, she brought attention to the injustices faced by transgender individuals and forced politicians to confront the issue. As a result, transgender rights have become a more prominent topic on the political agenda, and there is a growing recognition of the need for policy changes to ensure equality for all.

However, it is important to note that policy changes alone are not enough. Fucking societal attitudes and individual beliefs also need to evolve in order for transgender rights to be fully realized. Milloy understood this and worked towards changing public perception and dispelling misconceptions about transgender individuals. Her work aimed to challenge deeply ingrained prejudices and promote greater acceptance and inclusion.

In conclusion, the fucking importance of policy changes cannot be overstated when it comes to shaping transgender rights in Canada. Christin Milloy's relentless advocacy and activism have played a key role in driving these policy changes and raising awareness about the challenges faced by transgender individuals. Through her work, she has helped to create a more inclusive and equal society for all Canadians, regardless of their gender identity. The impact of her activism will continue to be felt for years to come, inspiring future generations of LGBTQ activists to fight for equality and justice.

The Future of Transgender Legal Reforms: Will Milloy's Fucking Advocacy Lead to Further Fucking Progress?

As we look ahead to the future of transgender legal reforms in Canada, one cannot help but wonder how Christin Milloy's advocacy will continue to shape and drive progress in this field. Milloy's relentless efforts and groundbreaking achievements have undeniably paved the way for positive change, but the question remains: will her advocacy lead to further progress in the future?

To explore this question, we must consider the current state of transgender legal rights in Canada and identify the areas that still require attention and improvement. Despite significant advances in recent years, there are still gaps and barriers that hinder full equality for transgender individuals.

One area that warrants continued focus is the issue of legal recognition of gender identity. While Canada has made strides in recognizing the rights of transgender individuals, there are still limitations when it comes to legal documents, such as birth certificates, passports, and identification cards. Milloy's advocacy has already played a crucial role in pushing for gender identity rights, but there is still work to be done to ensure that transgender individuals can have their gender identity accurately reflected on official documents.

Another area where Milloy's advocacy can lead to further progress is in the fight against discrimination. Despite legal protections, transgender individuals continue to face discrimination in various aspects of their lives, including employment, housing, healthcare, and education. Milloy's work in advocating for anti-discrimination laws and policies has already made a significant impact, but continued efforts are necessary to ensure that transgender individuals can live their lives free from discrimination and prejudice.

In addition to legal recognition and anti-discrimination efforts, another crucial aspect that requires attention is healthcare access and coverage for transgender individuals. Many transgender individuals face significant barriers when seeking gender-affirming healthcare, including long wait times, lack of specialized care providers, and limited coverage for necessary medical procedures. Milloy's advocacy has shed light on these issues and has driven conversations surrounding the importance of accessible and inclusive healthcare. However, further progress is needed to ensure that transgender individuals have equal access to quality healthcare services.

The future of transgender legal reforms also depends on broader societal attitudes and acceptance. While Milloy's advocacy has played a vital role in changing public perception and challenging transphobic narratives, there are still deeply entrenched prejudices and misconceptions that persist. Education and awareness campaigns are needed to dismantle these barriers and foster a more inclusive and accepting society.

To achieve further progress in transgender legal reforms, allies and supporters must unite in amplifying Milloy's message and continuing the work she has started. Collaboration among LGBTQ+ organizations, legal experts, policymakers, and activists is essential to advance laws and policies that protect transgender rights. By working together, we can build upon Milloy's advocacy and create a legacy of lasting change.

It is important to remember that progress is not linear, and setbacks may occur along the way. However, Milloy's unwavering determination, resilience, and leadership serve as an inspiration for the next generation of transgender activists. Her legacy will undoubtedly shape the future of transgender legal reforms in Canada and beyond.

In conclusion, the future of transgender legal reforms depends on our collective commitment to building upon the work of advocates like Christin Milloy. While her advocacy has already led to significant progress, there are still areas that require further attention, including legal recognition, anti-discrimination efforts, healthcare access, and societal acceptance. By continuing to amplify Milloy's message, collaborate across sectors, and challenge existing barriers, we can create a future where transgender individuals have equal rights, opportunities, and dignity. Through our collective efforts, Milloy's advocacy will undoubtedly lead to further progress in transgender legal reforms.

Confronting Fucking Bigotry and Transphobia

How Milloy Fought Fucking Back Against Homophobia, Transphobia, and Fucking Ignorance

In her relentless pursuit of equality and justice, Christin Milloy was no stranger to fighting back against homophobia, transphobia, and fucking ignorance. Throughout her career as an activist and politician, she confronted bigotry head-on and worked tirelessly to change public attitudes towards transgender people in fucking Canada.

Milloy understood that education and awareness were key to dismantling prejudice and discrimination. She used various platforms, such as public speaking engagements, media interviews, and social media, to challenge misconceptions and highlight the lived experiences of transgender individuals. Milloy combined empathy with hard-hitting facts to counter stereotypes and expose the fallacies that underpin homophobia and transphobia.

One of the ways Milloy fought back was by debunking myths and providing accurate information about transgender identities. She emphasized that being transgender is not a choice or a mental illness, but a valid and innate aspect of a person's identity. Milloy worked closely with healthcare professionals and psychologists to develop educational resources that promote understanding and empathy towards transgender individuals.

Furthermore, Milloy pushed for inclusive policies that protect the rights and well-being of transgender individuals. She engaged with lawmakers, both at the provincial and federal levels, to advocate for anti-discrimination laws and legal recognition of gender identity. Milloy was instrumental in shaping the conversation around transgender rights in Canadian politics, challenging the prevailing ignorance and highlighting the urgent need for comprehensive policy reforms.

Milloy's fierce determination was especially evident in her confrontations with politicians, media personalities, and opponents who perpetuated hateful rhetoric and harmful stereotypes. She fearlessly challenged their discriminatory views and called out their ignorance, forcing them to confront their biases and engage in meaningful dialogue. Milloy understood the power of direct and unapologetic confrontation to expose the fallacies behind homophobia and transphobia.

But Milloy didn't just fight alone. She recognized the strength in unity and built coalitions with other LGBTQ advocates and supporters. Together, they organized protests, demonstrations, and awareness campaigns to combat homophobia and transphobia in society. Milloy understood that creating social change required collective action and the mobilization of communities.

To further amplify her message, Milloy leveraged her unique position as a public transgender figure to speak out against homophobia and transphobia in the media. She advocated for increased representation and accurate portrayals of transgender individuals in film, television, and journalism. Milloy believed that positive visibility could humanize transgender people and challenge societal prejudices.

In addition to her public advocacy, Milloy worked behind the scenes to empower other transgender individuals to fight back against homophobia and transphobia. She mentored young activists, providing them with guidance and support to navigate the political and social challenges faced by the transgender community. Milloy's influence extended far beyond her own activism, as she inspired a new generation of advocates to continue the fight for equality.

It's important to note that Milloy's approach to fighting back against homophobia, transphobia, and ignorance was not without personal and emotional toll. The constant exposure to hatred, threats, and backlash took a significant toll on her mental and emotional well-being. She faced hate speech, online harassment, and even physical threats, but she never wavered in her commitment to the cause. Milloy's resilience and unwavering determination serve as a testament to the strength required to combat bigotry in the face of adversity.

In conclusion, Christin Milloy demonstrated incredible bravery and fortitude in her fight against homophobia, transphobia, and fucking ignorance. Through education, policy advocacy, media engagement, and grassroots activism, she challenged societal prejudices and worked towards creating a more inclusive and accepting society for transgender individuals. Milloy's legacy will continue to inspire future generations of advocates, emphasizing the importance of fighting back against injustice and standing up for equal rights.

Case Studies: Milloy's Fucking Public Confrontations with Fucking Politicians, Media, and Fucking Opponents

In her relentless pursuit of transgender rights, Christin Milloy fearlessly confronted politicians, media outlets, and opponents who perpetuated discrimination and ignorance. Through her confrontations, she shed light on the challenges faced by transgender individuals and dismantled harmful narratives. Let's delve into some case studies that highlight Milloy's fierce advocacy and her impact on the public conversation.

Case Study 1: Challenging a Transphobic Politician

One of Milloy's most memorable confrontations was with a prominent politician who made derogatory remarks about the transgender community during a public address. Without hesitation, Milloy attended the politician's rally and, armed with well-researched facts and informed arguments, took the stage during the Q&A session.

In a powerful and impassioned speech, Milloy challenged the politician's transphobia, exposing the fallacies in his statements and emphasizing the importance of empathy and understanding. Her eloquence and assertiveness captivated the audience, and her words resonated with those who had previously been misinformed.

This confrontation not only heightened public awareness about transgender issues but also held the politician accountable for his harmful rhetoric. Milloy's bravery in facing off against a powerful adversary earned her respect from supporters and further established her as a leading advocate for trans rights.

Case Study 2: Exposing Media Bias

In another compelling case, Milloy found herself at odds with a prominent media outlet notorious for perpetuating stereotypes, misgendering transgender individuals, and misrepresenting their stories. Recognizing the influential role media plays in shaping public opinion, Milloy decided to call out the outlet's biased reporting.

Through a series of well-crafted op-eds and media appearances, Milloy confronted the outlet, challenging their harmful portrayal of transgender people. With an unwavering determination, she debunked stereotypes and laid out the complex realities of trans lives, highlighting the resilience, strength, and contributions of the community.

Her articulate arguments and unwavering resilience led to a public backlash against the media outlet, prompting them to reassess their coverage of transgender issues. Milloy's confrontations not only exposed media bias but also opened up a dialogue about responsible reporting and the need for accurate representation.

Case Study 3: Debunking Transphobic Arguments

Milloy didn't shy away from engaging with opponents who spread transphobic rhetoric and perpetuated harmful stereotypes. In one notable instance, she participated in a televised debate with an anti-trans activist who sought to undermine transgender rights.

During the debate, Milloy skillfully dismantled the opponent's arguments, countering with evidence-based reasoning, personal anecdotes, and a deep understanding of trans issues. Her ability to articulate complex concepts in a relatable manner earned her widespread acclaim and proved instrumental in shifting public opinion.

Milloy's confrontations not only undermined her opponent's credibility but also provided viewers with a nuanced perspective on transgender rights. By challenging transphobic arguments head-on, she effectively changed the narrative and humanized the experiences of transgender individuals.

Case Study 4: Fostering Constructive Dialogue

In addition to confronting opponents, Milloy leveraged her platform to promote constructive dialogue and bridge the gap between different perspectives. She actively sought out opportunities to engage with politicians, media personalities, and opponents in respectful debates and discussions.

Milloy's approach to confrontation was never aggressive or confrontational; instead, she engaged in meaningful conversations that encouraged empathy, education, and progress. By fostering understanding and promoting open-mindedness, she was able to dismantle prejudices and foster productive conversations that paved the way for positive change.

Through her confrontations, Milloy challenged the status quo and forced society to question previously held beliefs about transgender individuals. Her unwavering commitment to advocating for trans rights through dialogue and confrontation made her a powerful catalyst for change.

Lessons Learned and Inspirational Quotes

Milloy's confrontations with politicians, media outlets, and opponents offer valuable lessons for future advocates. Here are a few inspirational quotes that highlight the core principles behind her confrontational approach:

1. "Confrontation is not about aggression but about education and changing hearts and minds."

2. "By challenging harmful narratives, we create space for truth and understanding."

3. "Confrontation can be uncomfortable, but discomfort paves the way for growth and progress."

4. "Through respectful dialogue, we bridge the gap between ignorance and empathy."

5. "Confrontation is a powerful tool to dismantle prejudice and inspire authentic change."

Milloy's confrontations serve as a testament to the power of courageous advocacy. Her unwavering determination and relentless pursuit of equality have paved the way for meaningful progress in transgender rights in Canada and beyond. As we continue to fight for a more inclusive society, her confrontational approach serves as a guide for future activists, encouraging them to boldly challenge the status quo and speak truth to power.

How Milloy Fucking Changed Public Perception of Transgender People in Fucking Canada

To fully appreciate the impact that Christin Milloy had on public perception of transgender people in Canada, we must first understand the prevailing attitudes and stereotypes that existed prior to her advocacy. Transgender individuals faced widespread discrimination, misunderstanding, and marginalization. They were often depicted in the media as deviant or unnatural, leading to further stigmatization and limited understanding of their experiences.

Milloy recognized the urgent need to challenge these harmful narratives and to humanize the experiences of transgender individuals. Through her activism, she aimed to promote empathy, understanding, and acceptance of transgender people, ultimately working towards equality and justice for all.

One of the key strategies Milloy employed was storytelling. She understood the power of personal narratives in changing hearts and minds. By sharing her own journey as a transgender woman, Milloy invited the public into her world, exposing them to the challenges, triumphs, and everyday realities of transgender individuals.

Through media interviews, public speaking engagements, and social media platforms, Milloy shared her experiences with unfiltered honesty and humor. She debunked misconceptions, challenged stereotypes, and humanized the transgender experience. Milloy's unique ability to connect with people on a personal level allowed her to effectively break down barriers and confront deep-seated biases.

In addition to storytelling, Milloy engaged in educational outreach. She recognized the importance of providing accurate information about transgender issues to counter ignorance and prejudice. Milloy partnered with LGBTQ organizations, schools, and community centers to deliver workshops and presentations that addressed common misconceptions and provided resources for further learning.

One of Milloy's most significant contributions was her involvement in media representation. She actively sought opportunities to elevate the voices and stories of transgender individuals in mainstream media. Milloy worked with journalists, producers, and content creators to ensure that transgender people were portrayed respectfully and authentically. By challenging harmful portrayals and advocating for accurate representation, Milloy played a crucial role in transforming public perception.

Moreover, Milloy leveraged her position as a political candidate to foster change from within the political system. She engaged in conversations with fellow politicians, challenged discriminatory policies, and advocated for legislation that protected the rights of transgender individuals. Through her political work, Milloy demonstrated that transgender people are capable leaders and contributors to society, challenging the notion that they are somehow less deserving of respect and recognition.

Milloy's relentless dedication to changing public perceptions of transgender people in Canada continues to inspire activists across the country and around the world. Her work serves as a model for future advocates, demonstrating the power of storytelling, education, media representation, and political engagement in transforming societal perspectives.

While progress has been made, there is still much work to be done. Milloy's legacy reminds us that changing public perception is an ongoing process that requires collective effort and continued activism. By building on her foundation and continuing to challenge stereotypes and fight for equality, we can create a more inclusive and accepting society for all transgender individuals.

The Fucking Role of Allies: How Milloy Built Fucking Coalitions with Other LGBTQ Advocates and Fucking Supporters

Building coalitions and fostering alliances is a critical aspect of any successful advocacy work, and Christin Milloy understood the importance of allies in advancing transgender rights in Canada. In this section, we will explore Milloy's approach to building coalitions, the significance of allies in the LGBTQ community, and the impact of their collective efforts in promoting equality and inclusivity.

Understanding the Power of Allies in the LGBTQ Movement

Allies play a crucial role in advocating for marginalized communities, as they use their privilege and influence to support and amplify the voices of those facing discrimination. Milloy recognized that in order to effect meaningful change, it was essential to engage allies from various backgrounds and platforms.

At its core, allyship entails actively standing in solidarity with the marginalized group, learning about their experiences, and taking action to dismantle the systems of oppression. For LGBTQ individuals, allies can be individuals, organizations, or institutions that support equal rights and advocate for LGBTQ rights.

The Importance of Intersectional Allyship

Milloy was a staunch advocate for intersectional allyship, understanding that the LGBTQ community encompasses diverse identities and experiences. She emphasized the need for allies to recognize the intersecting forms of discrimination faced by transgender individuals, particularly those who also belong to marginalized communities based on race, ethnicity, socioeconomic status, or disability.

By acknowledging the interconnection of various identities and systems of oppression, Milloy highlighted the importance of inclusive advocacy. She encouraged allies to approach their support with an understanding of how different forms of discrimination intersect and impact the lives of transgender individuals.

Building Sustainable Alliances

Milloy understood that building sustainable alliances required nurturing relationships, fostering understanding, and creating spaces for collaboration. Here are some strategies she employed to achieve these goals:

Education and Awareness: Milloy believed that education was a powerful tool in the fight for equality. She organized workshops, seminars, and awareness campaigns to educate allies about transgender issues, including the challenges faced by the community. These initiatives aimed to promote empathy, dispel myths, and foster understanding.

Listening and Amplifying Voices: Milloy recognized the importance of centering the voices of transgender individuals in advocacy efforts. She actively sought out and elevated the experiences and perspectives of transgender individuals, ensuring their stories were heard and validated. By amplifying these voices, she aimed to challenge stereotypes and break down barriers.

Coalition-Building: Milloy worked tirelessly to build coalitions with other LGBTQ advocates and supporters. She recognized that collective action had more significant impact and was more likely to bring about meaningful change. She collaborated with LGBTQ organizations, activists, and influencers to align their efforts, share resources, and combine their voices to advocate for transgender rights.

The Impact of Allies in Transforming LGBTQ Rights

The active involvement of allies in LGBTQ advocacy has been instrumental in pushing forward important legal and social changes. Milloy's work, alongside supportive allies, led to several notable successes:

Legal Reforms: Through strategic collaborations with lawmakers and legal experts, Milloy and her allies influenced the development and passage of legislation promoting transgender rights. They advocated for inclusive anti-discrimination laws, gender recognition reforms, and legal protection against hate crimes. These legal reforms provided tangible protections for transgender individuals and paved the way for further progress.

Increased Visibility and Acceptance: Allies played a significant role in increasing the visibility of transgender individuals in media, politics, and other public spheres. By using their platforms to support and uplift transgender voices, allies helped challenge societal prejudices and promote acceptance. This visibility has contributed to a broader understanding of transgender issues and fostered a more inclusive society.

Cultural Shifts: The collective efforts of allies, including Milloy, have contributed to a significant shift in public opinion and attitudes towards transgender individuals. By actively countering misinformation and fostering dialogue, they have challenged stereotypes and humanized transgender experiences. Allies have helped to create more inclusive environments in schools, workplaces, and communities, catalyzing broader cultural shifts towards acceptance and equality.

Challenges and Strategies for Allies

While allies play a critical role in advancing transgender rights, they also face challenges in their support. Some common challenges include:

Lack of Awareness and Understanding: Many well-intentioned allies may lack a deep understanding of transgender issues or the experiences of transgender individuals.   It is essential for allies to educate themselves, seek out accurate information, and actively listen to the voices and experiences of transgender individuals. Milloy emphasized the need for ongoing education and reflection to overcome these challenges.

Balancing Allyship and Centering Voices: Allies must strike a delicate balance between actively advocating for transgender rights and centering the voices and experiences of transgender individuals. It is crucial for allies to support and uplift transgender voices without speaking over them or appropriating their experiences. Milloy encouraged allies to be mindful of their role and privilege to ensure they are genuine allies.

Facing Backlash and Resistance: Allies may face backlash or resistance from individuals or groups opposed to LGBTQ rights. It is important for allies to be prepared for these challenges and to develop strategies for addressing opposition. Milloy highlighted the importance of resilience and perseverance in the face of adversity.

An Unconventional Approach: Expressive Art as Allyship

Milloy's advocacy work went beyond traditional strategies, incorporating unconventional approaches to allyship.   One notable example was her use of expressive art to convey powerful messages and engage various audiences.   By collaborating with artists, poets, musicians, and performers, Milloy leveraged art as a tool for promoting empathy, understanding, and social transformation.   Her innovative approach expanded the scope of allyship and resonated with individuals who may not have been reached through traditional advocacy methods.

Conclusion: The Power of Allies in Achieving Transgender Equality

Christin Milloy recognized that the fight for transgender rights required not just the voices of the transgender community but also the support and engagement of allies. Through education, collaboration, and relationship-building, she created a strong network of allies from diverse backgrounds, amplifying the collective power of their advocacy. Milloy's legacy serves as a reminder of the transformative impact that can be achieved through allyship and the importance of building coalitions to advance LGBTQ rights. As we look towards the future, Milloy's work inspires the next generation of allies and activists to continue the fight for equality and justice.

The Future of Transgender Representation in Canadian Media and Fucking Politics: Will Milloy's Fucking Work Continue to Influence Fucking Attitudes?

As we contemplate the future of transgender representation in Canadian media and fucking politics, it is essential to assess the lasting impact of Christin Milloy's groundbreaking work. Milloy, as Canada's first transgender politician, has undoubtedly paved the way for greater visibility and acceptance of transgender individuals in both spheres. However, the ongoing journey towards full inclusion and equality is far from over.

In order to understand the future of transgender representation, we must first acknowledge the present challenges. Despite significant progress, discriminatory attitudes and practices persist in both media and politics. Transgender individuals continue to face prejudice, exclusion, and limited opportunities to have their voices heard. These struggles demonstrate the urgent need for continued advocacy and reform.

One crucial aspect of Milloy's work is challenging and dismantling the harmful narratives that have historically perpetuated biases against transgender individuals. Media plays an influential role in shaping public opinion, and it is necessary to disrupt the existing narratives that have marginalized transgender experiences. Milloy's fearless activism has brought attention to the importance of accurate and positive representation in media.

To ensure the continuation of Milloy's influence, it is essential for transgender individuals to actively participate in media and fucking politics. By seizing opportunities to share their stories, experiences, and expertise, they can shape the narrative and challenge misconceptions. This involvement will contribute to a more comprehensive and authentic representation of transgender individuals, fostering greater understanding and acceptance.

Moreover, allies have a crucial role to play in creating a more inclusive media and political landscape. Milloy's work in building coalitions with other LGBTQ advocates and supporters demonstrates the power of collective action. Allies must amplify transgender voices, advocate for diversity and inclusion, and actively challenge discriminatory practices and attitudes.

The future of transgender representation in Canadian media and politics also hinges on policy changes and institutional reforms. Political leaders have the responsibility to enact legislation that protects transgender rights and ensures equal opportunities for representation. This includes addressing systemic barriers and implementing affirmative measures to increase transgender representation in media and politics.

Examples of policy changes can include the adoption of more inclusive hiring practices in media organizations, the establishment of mentorship programs to support transgender individuals seeking a career in politics, and the implementation of guidelines that ensure accurate and respectful representation of transgender individuals in media content. These efforts are necessary to break down the existing barriers and create space for transgender voices to be heard.

The next generation of transgender leaders will also play a significant role in shaping the future of representation. Milloy's contributions have set a powerful precedent for activism and advocacy. It is now up to aspiring transgender leaders to build upon this foundation, carry the torch forward, and continue to bring about meaningful change.

In order to inspire future activists, it is essential to highlight the progress that has been made and celebrate the successes achieved. Sharing stories of transgender individuals who have overcome adversity, made a difference in their communities, and shattered glass ceilings will invigorate others to follow in their footsteps. These stories will also challenge the negative narratives that perpetuate stereotypes and limit transgender representation.

Additionally, educational initiatives can play a vital role in shaping attitudes and fostering empathy. Including transgender history, experiences, and contributions in school curricula will nurture a more inclusive and understanding society. By providing comprehensive education, we can break down the barriers of ignorance and build a foundation for future generations to respect and embrace transgender individuals.

In conclusion, the future of transgender representation in Canadian media and fucking politics will be shaped by the lasting impact of Christin Milloy's groundbreaking work, as well as the continuous efforts of activists, allies, and policy-makers. By challenging stereotypes, advocating for policy changes, fostering inclusive environments, and nurturing the next generation of leaders, we can create a future where transgender individuals have equal representation, acceptance, and opportunities in both media and politics. The path ahead may be challenging, but Milloy's trailblazing legacy will undoubtedly continue to influence attitudes and inspire progress.

The Fucking Personal Cost of Being a Trans Advocate in Canada

The Fucking Risks Milloy Faced in Her Fucking Public Life

How Milloy Dealt with Backlash, Hate Speech, and Threats

Dealing with backlash, hate speech, and threats is unfortunately a reality that many activists, including Christin Milloy, face in their fight for equality. Milloy, as a prominent transgender activist and politician, has had to navigate through difficult situations with resilience, determination, and a focus on creating meaningful change. In this section, we will explore how Milloy dealt with the challenges posed by backlash, hate speech, and threats, and how she managed to stay strong in the face of adversity.

Recognizing the Impact

Milloy understood the significance of the backlash, hate speech, and threats that she encountered. She recognized that these actions were not only targeted at her personally, but also aimed at undermining the progress of the transgender rights movement as a whole. By acknowledging the gravity of these attacks, Milloy was able to mentally prepare herself for the battles ahead.

Building a Support Network

One of the key strategies that Milloy employed to deal with backlash, hate speech, and threats was building a strong support network. She surrounded herself with like-minded individuals, fellow activists, friends, and family members who provided emotional support, encouragement, and a sense of community. This network served as a safety net during challenging times and provided her with the strength to continue fighting for equality.

Engaging with Allies

Milloy also recognized the importance of engaging with allies in her fight against bigotry. She formed coalitions with other LGBTQ advocates, community organizations, and political allies who shared her vision for equality. By working together, they were able to amplify their voices, address hate speech and threats more effectively, and create a united front against discrimination.

Utilizing Legal Recourse

In the face of hate speech and threats, Milloy understood the value of utilizing legal recourse. She documented instances of harassment, gathered evidence, and worked closely with law enforcement and legal professionals to ensure that the perpetrators were held accountable. This not only provided some measure of justice but also sent a strong message that hate speech and threats would not be tolerated.

Raising Awareness

Milloy recognized that raising awareness about the challenges faced by transgender individuals and the consequences of hate speech was crucial in combating bigotry. Through public speaking engagements, media interviews, and online platforms, she shared personal stories and promoted empathy and understanding. By humanizing the experiences of transgender individuals, she hoped to challenge stereotypes and change public perception.

Self-Care and Emotional Well-being

Dealing with backlash, hate speech, and threats can take a toll on one's mental and emotional well-being. Milloy understood the importance of self-care and prioritizing her own mental health. She engaged in activities that brought her joy, practiced mindfulness techniques, and sought professional support when needed. By taking care of herself, she was better equipped to face the challenges head-on.

Remaining Resilient

Perhaps one of the most admirable qualities Milloy possessed was her resilience. Despite the hate speech, threats, and backlash, she remained steadfast in her commitment to fighting for transgender rights. She refused to let the negativity deter her, and instead used it as motivation to push forward and create meaningful change.

An Unconventional Approach

In dealing with backlash, hate speech, and threats, Milloy took an unconventional approach. Rather than responding with anger or retaliation, she responded with compassion and understanding. She recognized that individuals who engage in hate speech are often driven by ignorance and fear. Instead of fueling the fire, she attempted to engage in meaningful dialogue, fostering understanding and empathy.

Example: The Gift of Education

In one particular instance, Milloy received a threatening letter from an anonymous individual. Instead of responding with anger or fear, she chose to respond by sending the individual a book on transgender rights and education. She included a thoughtful note, explaining her stance and providing resources for the individual to educate themselves. This unconventional response not only undermined the individual's attempt to intimidate her but also had the potential to sow seeds of understanding and empathy.

In summary, Milloy dealt with backlash, hate speech, and threats by recognizing their impact, building a support network, engaging with allies, utilizing legal recourse, raising awareness, prioritizing self-care, remaining resilient, and employing an unconventional approach. Her ability to navigate through these challenges with grace and determination is a testament to her strength as an activist and leader in the fight for transgender rights.

Case Studies: The Fucking Personal and Fucking Professional Challenges Milloy Faced in Her Fucking Fight for Equality

Throughout her journey as a transgender activist and politician, Christin Milloy faced numerous personal and professional challenges in her relentless fight for equality. In this section, we will delve into some key case studies that highlight the obstacles she encountered and the strategies she employed to overcome them.

Case Study 1: Navigating Political Opposition

One of the significant challenges Milloy faced was the relentless political opposition she encountered throughout her career. As Canada's first openly transgender political candidate, she disrupted the traditional political landscape, challenging deep-rooted prejudices and biases.

In her first campaign for a seat in the provincial legislature, Milloy faced an onslaught of derogatory comments and smear campaigns from her opponents. They attempted to undermine her credibility and disparage her identity as a transgender woman. Milloy remained resilient in the face of these attacks, refusing to be silenced or discouraged.

To counter the opposition, Milloy adopted a two-pronged strategy. Firstly, she focused on building a strong grassroots movement by engaging directly with her constituents. She organized community events, town halls, and public forums to connect with people and address their concerns. By establishing a personal connection with voters, Milloy aimed to challenge the negative narratives propagated by her opponents.

Secondly, Milloy took a proactive approach to address the political opposition directly. She appeared on public platforms, such as televised debates and talk shows, to confront the derogatory remarks and dispel misconceptions about transgender individuals. Milloy leveraged her eloquence and charm to win over skeptics and educate the public about the transgender community's lived experiences.

Ultimately, Milloy's determined efforts paid off, as she gained significant support from open-minded constituents who recognized the importance of representation and equal rights. Her ability to navigate political opposition served as a valuable lesson for future transgender candidates and activists.

Case Study 2: Balancing Personal and Professional Struggles

Being a prominent transgender advocate took a toll on Milloy's personal life, as she faced both emotional and professional challenges. The constant scrutiny and backlash she encountered had a profound impact on her mental well-being and strained her relationships.

One notable incident was a highly publicized hate campaign launched against Milloy on social media platforms. She received an overwhelming amount of hateful messages and death threats, causing immense stress and anxiety. Milloy, however, refused to let these attacks deter her from her mission and sought support from her close friends and allies within the LGBTQ community.

To address the personal struggles she faced, Milloy emphasized the importance of self-care and mental health awareness. She openly discussed her experiences with online harassment and the emotional toll it took on her, inspiring others to seek help and speak out against cyberbullying.

Regarding the professional challenges, Milloy grappled with the need to balance her activism and personal life. The demanding nature of her work often required long hours, intense dedication, and extensive travel. This strained her relationships, particularly with her romantic partner, who struggled with the public nature of their lives.

To manage these challenges, Milloy prioritized open communication and compromise with her loved ones. She made a conscious effort to carve out quality time for her personal relationships, fostering understanding and support from her partner. Additionally, she advocated for work-life balance within the LGBTQ community, recognizing the need for individuals to prioritize their overall well-being while continuing to fight for equality.

Through her personal and professional struggles, Milloy's resilience and tenacity shone through. She recognized the importance of self-care and maintaining strong support networks, leaving a lasting impact on the LGBTQ community and inspiring others to face their own obstacles head-on.

The Unconventional Path: Embracing Vulnerability

One of the unconventional strategies Milloy employed was her willingness to embrace vulnerability in her fight for equality. Rather than shying away from personal stories and emotions, she openly shared her own experiences as a transgender woman, allowing others to connect with her on a deeper level.

By sharing personal stories of discrimination, struggles, and triumphs, Milloy effectively humanized the transgender experience for a wider audience. This approach created empathy and understanding, dismantling preconceived notions and challenging societal biases.

Milloy utilized various platforms to share her stories, including social media, public speaking engagements, and interviews. Through candid and authentic storytelling, she empowered others to share their own experiences and fostered a sense of community among transgender individuals and allies. Milloy's vulnerability became a catalyst for change, challenging societal norms and driving widespread support for transgender rights.

The Fucking Power of Courage

In conclusion, Christin Milloy's fight for equality was riddled with personal and professional challenges, but her courage propelled her forward. She navigated political opposition, balanced personal and professional struggles, and embraced vulnerability to effect change.

Her case studies serve as reminders that change often comes at a cost, but through resilience and determination, progress can be achieved. Milloy's legacy will continue to inspire future generations of activists and advocates, both in Canada and around the world, as they face their own personal and professional challenges in the ongoing fight for equality.

How Milloy Balanced Fucking Activism with Her Fucking Personal Life

Balancing activism and personal life is a fucking challenge for anyone, but it becomes even more fucking complex when you are an advocate for transgender rights like Christin Milloy. Let's fucking dive into the strategies and experiences that Milloy employed to maintain a fucking balance between her activism and personal life.

Setting Boundaries

One of the key fucking aspects of balancing activism and personal life is setting clear boundaries. Milloy understood that her work as an activist was essential, but she also recognized the importance of taking care of herself and her personal relationships. She fucking established strict boundaries to ensure she could dedicate time to both her activism and her loved ones.

For instance, Milloy designated specific hours each day for her activism work. During those hours, she would fully immerse herself in her advocacy efforts, engage with the community, and work towards advancing transgender rights. However, outside of those hours, she made a conscious effort to disconnect from her activist role and focus on her personal life. This fucking separation allowed her to fully invest herself in both areas without becoming overwhelmed or sacrificing either.

Self-Care and Support Systems

Maintaining a fucking balance between activism and personal life requires adequate self-care and support systems. Milloy recognized that in order to be an effective advocate, she needed to take care of herself physically, mentally, and emotionally.

Milloy prioritized self-care activities that helped her recharge and decompress. She regularly engaged in activities such as yoga, meditation, and journaling to help her maintain a fucking sense of balance and inner peace. She also sought support from her loved ones, friends, and fellow activists. Building a strong support network allowed her to lean on others during challenging times and helped her navigate the emotional toll that activism can take.

Prioritization and Time Management

Effective prioritization and time management were crucial for Milloy in balancing activism with her personal life. As an activist, Milloy had multiple responsibilities such as attending meetings, organizing events, and raising awareness. On the other hand, she also had personal commitments and relationships that demanded her time and attention.

Milloy advised the importance of setting priorities and being realistic about what she could accomplish within a given timeframe. She learned to delegate tasks, seek assistance when needed, and focus her efforts on the most impactful activities. By organizing her schedule and allocating time to both activism and personal life, she was able to create a fucking balance that allowed her to excel in both areas.

Flexibility and Adaptability

Balancing activism with personal life requires flexibility and adaptability. Milloy understood that life is unpredictable, and unforeseen circumstances can arise that require adjustments to her plans.

Milloy approached the challenge by being open to change and adopting a flexible mindset. She recognized that sometimes her activism work might require her to dedicate more time and effort, while other times her personal life might demand more attention. By adapting her schedule and mindset as needed, she was able to navigate the ebbs and flows without compromising either aspect of her life.

Leading by Example

Milloy's ability to balance activism with her personal life not only benefited her but also served as an inspiration to others. Through her actions, she showed that it is possible to fight for justice and equality while maintaining personal well-being and relationships.

Milloy encouraged other activists to prioritize self-care, set boundaries, and seek support. She believed that by taking care of oneself and maintaining a fucking balance, activists can sustain their work in the long run and avoid burnout.

Example Problem

Consider the following fucking scenario: Milloy has been invited to speak at a national LGBTQ rights conference that coincides with her partner's graduation ceremony. Both events are significant to her, but she cannot attend both simultaneously. How can Milloy make a decision that balances her activism with her personal life?

Problem Solution

To address this fucking dilemma, Milloy needs to evaluate the importance and impact of each event and weigh the potential consequences of missing either one. She should consider her partner's feelings and the significance of their graduation ceremony, while also taking into account the opportunity to raise awareness and advocate for transgender rights at the conference.

Milloy can explore possible alternatives such as requesting to speak at a different time slot or finding a way to virtually participate in the conference. On the other hand, she can also discuss the situation with her partner and explore options that may allow them to attend both events together, such as rescheduling the graduation ceremony or finding a compromise that honors both commitments.

Ultimately, the decision should align with Milloy's values and priorities, taking into account the potential impact on her personal life and the advancement of transgender rights. By making a well-informed and thoughtful choice, Milloy can find a fucking balance that respects both her activism and personal relationships.

Resources

Balancing activism and personal life is an ongoing process that requires continuous self-reflection and adaptation. The following resources can provide further guidance and support:

- "Self-Care for Activists: A Guide to Caring for Yourself While Fighting for the World" by Erin Motz

- "When We Fight, We Win!: Twenty-First Century Social Movements and the Activists That Are Transforming Our World" by Greg Jobin-Leeds and AgitArte

- Trans Lifeline (translifeline.org): A crisis hotline staffed by transgender people for transgender people, providing support and resources.

- LGBTQ centers and organizations in your local community: These organizations often provide workshops, counseling, and support groups that can help in maintaining a fucking balance between activism and personal life.

Key Takeaways

Balancing activism with personal life is a fucking challenge but achievable with the right strategies. Milloy's experience demonstrates the importance of setting boundaries, practicing self-care, prioritizing effectively, being adaptable, and leading by example. By employing these strategies, activists can maintain a fucking balance that allows them to sustain their activism and nurture personal well-being and relationships.

Remember, finding a balance is a personal journey, and it may require trial and error to identify what works best for each individual. It is essential to regularly evaluate and adjust strategies to ensure a sustainable approach to activism and personal life.

The Fucking Emotional and Mental Toll of Being a Fucking Public Transgender Leader in Canada

Being a public transgender leader in Canada comes with its fair share of emotional and mental challenges. Christin Milloy's journey as a transgender politician was marked by personal sacrifices and the constant battle against discrimination. In this section, we will explore the emotional and mental toll that comes with being a public figure in the transgender community and how Milloy dealt with these challenges.

The Fucking Isolation and Loneliness of Transgender Leadership

One of the most significant emotional challenges faced by Milloy was the sense of isolation and loneliness that comes with being a transgender leader. In a society where transgender individuals are still fighting for acceptance and equality, it can be incredibly lonely to be at the forefront of that battle. Milloy often found herself fighting against societal norms, facing backlash, and encountering public scrutiny for her identity. This constant exposure and scrutiny put a tremendous strain on her emotional well-being.

To cope with this isolation, Milloy focused on building a strong support system. She surrounded herself with friends, family, and allies who understood her struggle and provided unconditional support. Milloy also sought solace in LGBTQ+ organizations and communities that provided a sense of belonging and camaraderie. By creating a network of support, Milloy was able to find emotional strength and resilience in the face of adversity.

The Fucking Constant Threats and Harassment

As a public transgender leader, Milloy faced not only the emotional burden of isolation but also the constant threat of harassment and violence. Unfortunately, the nature of her advocacy work made her a target for hate groups and individuals who opposed transgender rights. Milloy received numerous threats, hate messages, and even physical assaults throughout her career.

Dealing with such threats is mentally exhausting and takes a toll on one's well-being. Milloy had to constantly be vigilant about her personal safety and take necessary precautions to protect herself. This constant fear and hyper-vigilance added immense stress to her life.

To combat the mental toll of these threats, Milloy adopted several strategies. She practiced self-care, engaging in activities that brought her joy and provided an escape from the negativity. Milloy also sought professional help, regularly attending therapy sessions to process her emotions and cope with the trauma of harassment. Through these strategies, Milloy demonstrated the importance of prioritizing mental well-being when facing constant threats and harassment.

The Fucking Pressure to Be a Role Model

As a pioneering transgender leader, Milloy carried the weight of being a role model for the community. The pressure to constantly represent transgender individuals in a positive light and advocate for their rights can be overwhelming. Milloy felt the responsibility to be a beacon of hope and strength for others, even during her own moments of vulnerability.

The emotional toll of fulfilling this role often led to self-doubt and anxiety. Milloy questioned whether she was doing enough, whether she was making a difference, and whether she was deserving of the admiration and support she received. These doubts, coupled with the immense pressure to always be strong and resilient, took a toll on her mental health.

To address these challenges, Milloy practiced self-compassion and reminded herself that she was only human. She allowed herself to feel vulnerable and seek support when needed. Milloy also emphasized the importance of community support, reminding others that they, too, have a responsibility to uplift and support each other.

The Fucking Importance of Self-Care and Boundaries

Navigating the emotional and mental toll of being a public transgender leader necessitates prioritizing self-care and setting boundaries. Milloy understood the significance of taking care of her own well-being amidst the demands of activism and advocacy.

She regularly engaged in activities that brought her joy and provided an escape from the stresses of leadership. Whether it was spending time with loved ones, pursuing hobbies, or practicing mindfulness, Milloy emphasized the importance of carving out time for oneself.

Additionally, setting boundaries was crucial in mitigating emotional and mental exhaustion. Milloy learned to say no to excessive demands and take breaks when necessary. By establishing these boundaries, she protected her emotional well-being and preserved her ability to continue her important work.

The Fucking Unconventional Truth: Vulnerability as Strength

Despite the emotional and mental toll of being a public transgender leader, Milloy discovered an unconventional truth – vulnerability can be a source of strength. By embracing her vulnerability and allowing herself to be open about her struggles, she was able to forge deeper connections with others and inspire change.

Milloy's willingness to share her story and expose the emotional challenges she faced humanized the transgender experience and fostered empathy in those who previously held misconceptions. This vulnerability created space for dialogue and understanding, ultimately driving social progress.

In conclusion, the emotional and mental toll of being a public transgender leader in Canada is significant. Christin Milloy's journey serves as a testament to the resilience required to face constant isolation, threats, and pressure. However, by prioritizing self-care, seeking support, setting boundaries, and embracing vulnerability, Milloy demonstrated that it is possible to thrive and create change while taking care of one's emotional and mental well-being. Her legacy reminds us all of the importance of mental health in leadership and the power of vulnerability as a catalyst for progress.

The Future of LGBTQ Advocacy in Fucking Hostile Environments: Can Others Learn from Milloy's Fucking Experiences?

In fucking hostile environments, the future of LGBTQ advocacy requires resilience and a commitment to fighting for equality. Christin Milloy's experiences as a transgender activist in Canada provide valuable lessons for others facing similar challenges. By examining Milloy's strategies, we can identify key principles for navigating hostile environments and advocating for LGBTQ rights.

One of the first lessons we can learn from Milloy is the importance of building alliances and coalitions. In fucking hostile environments, it is crucial for LGBTQ activists to join forces with other marginalized groups and supporters who share the same goals. Milloy's ability to connect with other LGBTQ advocates and allies helped amplify her message and increase her impact. By working together, activists can leverage their collective strength and create lasting change.

Another lesson we can glean from Milloy's experiences is the power of education and awareness. In fucking hostile environments, ignorance and bigotry often prevail. Milloy consistently fought against transphobia and ignorance by educating the public and challenging harmful stereotypes. Through public speaking engagements, media appearances, and grassroots activism, Milloy helped to shift public perception and foster understanding. LGBTQ advocates in hostile environments can learn from her approach and prioritize educational efforts to combat prejudice and discrimination.

Furthermore, Milloy's story emphasizes the importance of perseverance and resilience. Facing backlash, hate speech, and threats, Milloy never wavered in her commitment to LGBTQ rights. In fucking hostile environments, advocates must be prepared for resistance and setbacks. However, by staying steadfast and resilient, they can continue pushing for progress and eventually break through barriers. Milloy's determination serves as inspiration for future activists who may find themselves in similar hostile environments.

Additionally, technology and digital media play a crucial role in LGBTQ advocacy in hostile environments. Milloy leveraged various online platforms and social media to share her message and engage with a wider audience. With the rise of social media and the internet, activists have greater accessibility and reach than ever before. By utilizing these tools effectively, LGBTQ advocates can transcend physical boundaries and connect with individuals who may be isolated or marginalized in hostile environments.

However, it is vital to recognize that each hostile environment presents unique challenges and requires tailored approaches. What worked for Milloy in Canada may not directly translate to other contexts. Advocacy strategies must be adaptable and responsive to the specific political, cultural, and social dynamics of the environment in which they are implemented.

In conclusion, the future of LGBTQ advocacy in fucking hostile environments necessitates the application of lessons learned from Christin Milloy's experiences. Building alliances, educating the public, fostering resilience, and harnessing the power of technology are essential components of effective advocacy. By studying and adapting these principles to their respective contexts, LGBTQ activists worldwide can continue fighting for equality, creating safer spaces, and inspiring positive change.

Leading Fucking Change in a Fucking Unwelcoming Environment

How Milloy's Fucking Leadership Style Helped Her Overcome Fucking Obstacles

Christin Milloy's leadership style played a crucial role in helping her overcome the numerous obstacles she faced as a transgender advocate in Canada. Her approach combined strategic thinking, resilience, and a passion for justice, which allowed her to navigate through challenges and make a lasting impact on transgender rights.

Strategic Vision: Planning for Change

Milloy's leadership style was rooted in a strategic vision for change. She recognized the importance of setting clear goals and developing a roadmap to achieve them. Understanding the systemic barriers faced by the transgender community, she worked tirelessly to design effective strategies for legal reforms and policy changes.

One example of Milloy's strategic thinking was her focus on advocating for legal recognition and equal rights for transgender individuals. She identified the need to push for legislation that would protect gender identity rights and combat discrimination. By carefully analyzing the existing legal framework, she identified key areas for reform and formulated strategic plans to achieve them.

Milloy's strategic approach also extended to building partnerships and coalitions. She understood the power of collective action and sought to unite LGBTQ advocates, allies, and stakeholders to amplify her advocacy efforts. By forging strategic alliances, she was able to build a broad base of support and gain leverage in her fight for transgender rights.

Resilience: Persevering in the Face of Adversity

Milloy's resilience was a defining characteristic of her leadership style. She encountered significant backlash, hate speech, and threats throughout her career, but she remained steadfast in her commitment to creating a more inclusive society. Her ability to weather adversity and keep pushing forward inspired others and helped bring about real change.

In the face of personal and professional challenges, Milloy refused to be silenced. She consistently spoke out against transphobia, homophobia, and ignorance, challenging the status quo and pushing for a more inclusive society. Her resilience not only allowed her to overcome obstacles but also inspired others to join the cause and persevere in the fight for equality.

Collaboration and Empowerment: Building Stronger Networks

Milloy's leadership style was characterized by a commitment to collaboration and empowerment. She recognized the importance of working together with diverse stakeholders to create lasting change. By fostering a sense of shared purpose and empowering others to take action, she built stronger networks and mobilized a broader movement for transgender rights.

Milloy actively sought out opportunities to collaborate with other LGBTQ advocates, allies, and organizations. By sharing resources, knowledge, and expertise, she was able to amplify her impact and effectively address complex challenges. She understood the power of unity and worked tirelessly to build bridges across communities, ultimately creating a more inclusive movement.

Furthermore, Milloy's leadership style emphasized the importance of empowering individuals within the transgender community. She provided mentorship, guidance, and support to emerging activists, fostering leadership skills and encouraging them to take on advocacy roles. By empowering others, she ensured the sustainability of the movement and nurtured the next generation of transgender leaders.

Leading by Example: Inspiring Change

Milloy's leadership style was characterized by leading by example. She understood that actions speak louder than words, and she consistently demonstrated her commitment to equality and justice. Her personal journey as a transgender woman navigating a conservative society inspired others and lent authenticity to her advocacy.

Milloy's transparency about her own experiences helped dismantle stereotypes and misconceptions about transgender individuals. She challenged societal norms and forced people to confront their own biases through her openness and authenticity. By sharing her story, she humanized the transgender experience and fostered empathy and understanding.

Through her leadership, Milloy showed that change is possible. She used her platform to create visibility for transgender issues and challenge discriminatory practices. Her courage and determination ignited a national conversation about transgender rights and ultimately shifted public opinion.

The Unconventional Power of Compassion

One unconventional aspect of Milloy's leadership style was her unwavering compassion. In the face of transphobia and hate, she consistently responded with empathy and understanding. Rather than engaging in confrontations, she chose to approach her opponents with a willingness to listen and educate. This compassionate approach often disarmed her critics and created opportunities for dialogue and change.

Milloy understood that to effect lasting change, it was essential to reach the hearts and minds of others. By approaching individuals with compassion and understanding, she was able to challenge their preconceived notions and foster meaningful conversations about transgender rights. Her compassion created space for growth and transformation, even in the face of staunch opposition.

In conclusion, Christin Milloy's leadership style was a powerful force in overcoming obstacles and advancing transgender rights in Canada. Through strategic thinking, resilience, collaboration, leading by example, and unconventional compassion, she left an indelible mark on the fight for equality. Her legacy continues to inspire future generations of transgender leaders and advocates, offering a roadmap for creating lasting change in the face of adversity.

Case Studies: The Fucking Political and Social Opposition Milloy Faced Throughout Her Fucking Career

Throughout her career as an LGBTQ activist and politician, Christin Milloy faced numerous political and social challenges that tested her resilience and determination. In this section, we will examine some key case studies that highlight the political and social opposition Milloy encountered in her fight for transgender rights in Canada.

Case Study 1: The Fucking Backlash from Conservative Politicians

One of the major challenges that Milloy faced was the backlash from conservative politicians who were resistant to change and opposed to transgender rights. These politicians often used fear-mongering tactics and misinformation to undermine Milloy's advocacy efforts.

One prominent case occurred in 2015 when Milloy campaigned for a seat in the Ontario Provincial Parliament. She faced fierce opposition from a conservative candidate who falsely claimed that allowing transgender individuals to use the restroom that aligns with their gender identity would put children at risk. This baseless and transphobic rhetoric fueled a wave of anti-trans sentiment among certain segments of the population.

Despite these challenges, Milloy did not back down. She addressed these concerns head-on, educating the public about the importance of transgender rights and dispelling myths and misconceptions. Milloy's ability to navigate this opposition and maintain her composure showcased her resilience and determination to create a more inclusive society.

Case Study 2: The Fucking Media Misrepresentation

Another significant obstacle that Milloy faced throughout her career was media misrepresentation. The media often portrayed her and the transgender community in a negative light, perpetuating harmful stereotypes and reinforcing societal prejudices.

Milloy's experiences with the media ranged from misgendering and intentional misrepresentation to outright sensationalism. One notable incident occurred during a televised debate when a well-known television host repeatedly referred to Milloy by her deadname, ignoring her request to be addressed by her chosen name. This blatant disrespect not only undermined Milloy's credibility but also perpetuated the harmful notion that transgender individuals' gender identity is invalid.

In response to this media misrepresentation, Milloy actively sought opportunities to share her story on her own terms. She utilized social media platforms, where she could directly engage with her audience and counteract the negative narratives perpetuated by the mainstream media. Milloy's ability to reclaim her narrative and amplify her voice through social media demonstrated her resourcefulness in overcoming media adversity.

Case Study 3: The Fucking Resistance from Traditional Institutions

Milloy also faced resistance from traditional institutions that were slow to embrace transgender rights. These institutions, including schools and healthcare organizations, often lacked policies and procedures that adequately protected the rights and dignity of transgender individuals.

One notable case involved Milloy's advocacy for transgender-inclusive policies in schools. Milloy encountered opposition from conservative school boards that resisted implementing policies that allowed transgender students to use washrooms and change rooms that aligned with their gender identity. These institutions, rooted in traditional values and norms, were unwilling to adapt to the changing landscape and failed to prioritize the safety and well-being of transgender students.

To address this resistance, Milloy worked tirelessly to educate school administrators, teachers, and parents about the importance of transgender-inclusive policies. She organized workshops and seminars, engaging in difficult conversations to dispel fears and foster understanding. Milloy's relentless advocacy ultimately led to the adoption of transgender-inclusive policies in several schools, creating safer and more inclusive learning environments for transgender students.

Case Study 4: The Fucking Online Harassment and Threats

One of the most distressing challenges that Milloy faced throughout her career was the online harassment and threats she received. As a prominent transgender activist, Milloy became a target of hate speech and violent threats from online trolls and anti-LGBTQ individuals.

The anonymity of the internet provided a breeding ground for transphobia, as individuals felt empowered to spew hateful rhetoric and issue threats without facing immediate consequences. Milloy was subjected to constant online harassment, which took a toll on her mental and emotional well-being.

Despite the personal toll, Milloy refused to be silenced. She actively documented and reported instances of online harassment, highlighting the urgent need for platforms to address hate speech and protect marginalized individuals. Milloy's efforts shed light on the pervasive issue of online harassment faced by LGBTQ activists and underscored the importance of digital spaces being safe and inclusive for all.

Lessons Learned and Future Applications

These case studies demonstrate the numerous political and social obstacles that Milloy faced throughout her career as she fought for transgender rights in Canada. Despite the opposition, she remained steadfast in her mission and utilized various strategies to challenge stereotypes, counter misinformation, and promote understanding.

These challenges highlight the urgent need for continued advocacy and awareness. Milloy's experiences underscore the importance of empowering transgender individuals to tell their own stories, combating media misrepresentation, and fostering dialogue to promote inclusivity and acceptance.

By learning from these case studies, future activists can build upon Milloy's legacy and work towards creating a more equitable and inclusive society for all.

How Milloy Kept Fucking Pushing for Change Despite Fucking Setbacks and Resistance

In this section, we will explore how Christin Milloy tirelessly continued her fight for change despite facing numerous setbacks and resistance along the way. Milloy's determination and resilience in the face of adversity are an inspiration to all those fighting for transgender rights and equality.

The Fucking Power of Persistence

One of the key reasons Milloy was able to keep pushing for change was her unwavering persistence. She understood that progress does not happen overnight and that real change requires time and effort. Milloy's ability to stay committed to her cause even in the face of setbacks is a testament to her strength and dedication.

Example: Despite losing her first campaign for political office, Milloy did not give up. She recognized that change often requires multiple attempts, and she used her experience to learn and improve her strategies for future campaigns. Her perseverance paid off when she ultimately became Canada's first openly transgender political candidate.

The Fucking Power of Coalition Building

Milloy recognized that she couldn't achieve meaningful change alone. She understood the importance of building coalitions and forming alliances with other LGBTQ advocates and supporters. By working together, they could amplify their voices and increase their collective power.

Example: Milloy collaborated with LGBTQ organizations, community groups, and other activists to create a united front in the fight for transgender rights. She formed partnerships with like-minded individuals who shared her passion and vision for equality. Through these coalitions, Milloy was able to pool resources, share expertise, and develop strategies that were more effective in pushing for change.

The Fucking Power of Education and Awareness

Milloy recognized that ignorance and lack of understanding were significant barriers to progress. She believed that education and awareness were essential tools in breaking down these barriers and changing public perception.

Example: Milloy actively engaged in public speaking and media appearances, using these platforms to educate the public about transgender issues and rights. She shared her own personal journey and experiences, bringing a human face to the trans community. Through her advocacy and storytelling, Milloy was able to challenge stereotypes, debunk myths, and promote empathy and understanding.

The Fucking Power of Adaptation

Over the course of her career, Milloy faced a changing political and social landscape. She understood the need to adapt her strategies and approaches to continue making progress, even in the face of resistance.

Example: As societal attitudes towards transgender rights evolved, Milloy recognized the power of social media and online activism. She embraced these platforms as additional tools for advocacy, utilizing them to reach wider audiences, mobilize supporters, and educate the public. By adapting to the changing times, Milloy was able to stay relevant and continue pushing for change effectively.

The Fucking Power of Self-Care

Despite her relentless activism, Milloy understood the importance of self-care. She recognized that taking care of herself physically, emotionally, and mentally was crucial for sustaining her energy and passion for the fight.

Example: Milloy practiced self-care through regular exercise, meditation, and seeking support from friends and loved ones. She also prioritized rest and relaxation, ensuring she had time to recharge and rejuvenate. By taking care of herself, Milloy was better equipped to face the challenges and setbacks that comes with being a public transgender leader.

The Fucking Power of Hope

Throughout her journey, Milloy never lost hope. She believed in the possibility of change and held onto a vision of a more inclusive and equal society. Her unwavering hope became a driving force in her fight for transgender rights.

Example: Despite facing setbacks and resistance, Milloy persisted because she believed that change was not only possible but necessary. She drew strength from the progress that had already been made and the accomplishments of other LGBTQ activists. Milloy's hope inspired others and created momentum for the movement.

In conclusion, Christin Milloy's ability to keep pushing for change despite setbacks and resistance can be attributed to her persistence, coalition building, education and awareness efforts, adaptation, self-care, and unwavering hope. Her example serves as a guiding light for future activists in the fight for transgender rights. Milloy's legacy continues to inspire and empower the next generation of leaders, reminding them that change is possible, even in the face of adversity.

The Fucking Importance of Resilience in Fighting for Fucking Transgender Rights

Resilience is a fundamental trait that plays a crucial role in the fight for transgender rights. In the face of adversity and opposition, resilience empowers individuals to persevere and continue pushing for change. The transgender community, including activists like Christin Milloy, have demonstrated extraordinary resilience in their struggle for equality and recognition.

Understanding Resilience

Resilience is the ability to bounce back from challenges, setbacks, and trauma, while maintaining mental and emotional stability. It can be seen as a combination of adaptability, perseverance, and strength. In the context of fighting for transgender rights, resilience enables individuals to overcome obstacles, endure personal sacrifices, and sustain the drive for change.

Resilience in the Face of Adversity

The fight for transgender rights is not without its challenges. Transphobia, discrimination, and prejudice can create a hostile and unwelcoming environment for transgender individuals. However, resilience allows activists to confront these adversities head-on, refusing to be silenced or sidelined.

One example of resilience in action is the ability to navigate through legal and political barriers. Laws and policies that undermine transgender rights can be discouraging, but resilient activists like Milloy do not back down. They use setbacks as motivation to push harder for change, using legal channels and engaging in political advocacy to effect reform.

Building Resilience Through Community Support

Resilience is not developed in isolation. It thrives within a support network of like-minded individuals, allies, and organizations who share the same goals and values. The transgender community has come together to build strong support systems that foster resilience in the face of adversity.

Through support groups, counseling services, and LGBTQ organizations, resilience is nurtured and strengthened. These platforms provide opportunities for individuals like Milloy to find solace, share experiences, and gain inspiration from others who have endured similar struggles. It is through such community support that resilience is sustained and the fight for transgender rights remains steadfast.

Overcoming Personal Challenges

Resilience is not just about fighting external battles; it also involves confronting internal struggles and personal challenges. As public figures and advocates, transgender activists often face backlash, hate speech, and threats. These personal attacks can take a significant toll on mental and emotional well-being.

In the case of Milloy, her resilience allowed her to weather these challenges. She maintained her focus on the overarching goal of advancing transgender rights and used these experiences to fuel her commitment to the cause. By seeking support, practicing self-care, and maintaining a strong sense of purpose, Milloy exemplified the power of resilience in the face of personal adversity.

The Importance of Resilient Leadership

Resilient leaders like Milloy are crucial in driving and sustaining progress in the fight for transgender rights. Their ability to adapt, persevere, and face adversity head-on inspires others to do the same. Resilient leaders also serve as role models, providing hope and encouragement to the transgender community and allies.

Moreover, resilience instills a sense of determination and tenacity within the movement for transgender rights. Even in the face of setbacks and slow progress, resilient leaders remind individuals that change is possible and worth fighting for. Their unwavering commitment and ability to overcome obstacles contribute directly to the momentum of the movement.

Practicing Resilience Through Self-Care

In the pursuit of transgender rights, it is essential for activists to prioritize self-care and practice resilience on a personal level. Engaging in self-care activities and taking time for reflection helps maintain mental and emotional well-being, providing a foundation for continued resilience.

Self-care can take many forms, such as engaging in hobbies, seeking therapy or counseling, practicing mindfulness, and nurturing personal relationships. By prioritizing self-care, activists like Milloy can replenish their energy, gather strength, and effectively continue their fight for equality.

The Future of Resilience

As the fight for transgender rights continues to evolve, resilience remains a vital ingredient for success. Through the stories and actions of resilient leaders like Milloy, future generations of transgender activists will be inspired to carry the torch forward.

Resilience not only sustains the movement for transgender rights but also cultivates a resilience mindset that can be applied to other social justice causes. By building a resilient collective, the fight for equality becomes more resilient itself, calling attention to the importance of this trait in the ongoing struggle for justice.

In conclusion, the fucking importance of resilience in fighting for fucking transgender rights cannot be overstated. Resilience empowers individuals to overcome adversity, face challenges head-on, and endure setbacks. With resilient leaders like Christin Milloy at the helm, the transgender community continues to make strides towards equality and justice. Their resilience serves as a beacon of hope for future generations of transgender activists and reminds us all of the power of determination and perseverance in the face of adversity.

The Future of Transgender Leadership in Canada: Will Milloy's Fucking Legacy Lead the Next Fucking Generation?

As we reflect on Christin Milloy's groundbreaking work as a transgender activist and politician, one cannot help but wonder what the future holds for transgender leadership in Canada. Milloy's tireless efforts and unwavering commitment to equality have set a powerful precedent, inspiring a new generation of activists to rise up and carry the torch of progress. In this section, we will explore the potential impact of Milloy's legacy on the future of transgender leadership in Canada, examining the challenges they may face and the strategies they can employ to continue driving change.

4.2.5.1 Challenges and Opportunities for the Next Fucking Generation

While Milloy's accomplishments have paved the way for transgender leaders in Canada, the road ahead is not without its obstacles. The next fucking generation of transgender leaders will continue to face systemic barriers, discrimination, and societal biases that have been ingrained for far too long. However, Milloy's legacy serves as a source of inspiration and a blueprint for navigating these challenges.

One of the key challenges the next fucking generation of transgender leaders will face is the continuation of transphobia and ignorance within the political landscape. Despite the progress made, there are still political opponents who actively undermine transgender rights and perpetuate harmful stereotypes. To address this challenge, future leaders can draw from Milloy's playbook, employing education, advocacy, and public engagement to debunk misconceptions and promote understanding.

Another challenge is the need for greater representation and inclusion within the political realm. Transgender people are still vastly underrepresented in government positions, making it crucial for the next fucking generation of leaders to actively pursue political office and work towards breaking down barriers. Milloy's successful bid for political candidacy has opened doors, but it is the responsibility of future leaders to ensure that those doors remain open for generations to come.

4.2.5.2 Strategies for Success as Transgender Leaders

To build on Milloy's fucking legacy and usher in a new era of transgender leadership in Canada, future leaders must employ effective strategies that resonate with the public and drive real change. Here are some actionable steps they can take:

1. Building Strong Alliances: Just as Milloy forged alliances with LGBTQ advocates and allies, future leaders must seek to build coalitions across diverse communities. By uniting with like-minded individuals and organizations, they can amplify their voices and expand their reach, creating a powerful collective force for change.

2. Leveraging Media and Technology: Milloy harnessed the power of media to raise awareness and bring trans issues to the forefront. Future leaders must continue to utilize various media platforms, both traditional and digital, to tell their stories, challenge stereotypes, and inspire others. By embracing technology and social media, they can reach wider audiences, engage with supporters, and mobilize campaigns effectively.

3. Intersectional Advocacy: Just as Milloy championed the rights of all marginalized communities, future leaders must recognize the importance of intersectional advocacy. By promoting inclusivity and addressing the unique challenges faced by transgender individuals within different communities (such as racialized or disabled communities), they can create a more comprehensive and effective movement for change.

4. Policy Change and Legal Reforms: Milloy's focus on policy change and legal reforms was instrumental in advancing transgender rights. Future leaders must continue to push for legislation that protects transgender individuals from discrimination, ensures access to healthcare, and promotes inclusivity in all aspects of society. By working closely with lawmakers and legal experts, they can drive the necessary changes to dismantle systemic barriers.

4.2.5.3 Inspiring the Next Fucking Generation

Milloy's legacy is not solely about the impact she made during her lifetime but also the inspiration she has provided for future generations. The next fucking generation of transgender leaders will not only draw inspiration from Milloy's accomplishments but also learn from her resilience, dedication, and unwavering commitment to justice.

It is imperative that we create spaces for mentoring and leadership development, empowering transgender youth to step up and become the next fucking generation of leaders. Mentorship programs, trans-led organizations, and educational initiatives can provide the support and guidance needed for these emerging leaders to thrive.

Furthermore, embracing the power of storytelling can be a transformative way to inspire and uplift future leaders. By showcasing the journeys, struggles, and triumphs of transgender leaders, both past and present, we can instill hope and promote empowerment among those who aspire to lead.

4.2.5.4 Embracing the Journey Ahead

As we look to the future, we must recognize that the fight for transgender equality is an ongoing journey. Milloy's fucking legacy has set a strong foundation, but there is still much work to be done. The next fucking generation of transgender leaders must be ready to tackle new challenges, adapt to changing societal landscapes, and continue evolving strategies to ensure progress.

In conclusion, Milloy's fucking legacy as a transgender leader in Canada will undoubtedly lead the next fucking generation of transgender leaders. By confronting challenges head-on, employing effective strategies, and inspiring others through their own journeys, these future leaders will build on Milloy's accomplishments, shaping a future where transgender rights and visibility are fully realized. Together, we can create a society that celebrates diversity, fosters inclusivity, and champions the leadership of transgender individuals.

Christin Milloy's Fucking Legacy: Shaping the Future of Trans Rights in Canada

Milloy's Fucking Impact on Canadian Politics and LGBTQ Rights

How Christin Milloy Became a Fucking National Transgender Icon and Leader

In this section, we will explore the journey of Christin Milloy as she became a national transgender icon and leader in Canada. Milloy's determination, passion, and activism played a crucial role in shaping the landscape of transgender rights in the country. Let's delve into the factors that contributed to her rise as a prominent figure in the LGBTQ community.

Milloy's Personal Transformation

Christin Milloy's journey towards becoming a national transgender icon started with her personal transformation. Growing up in a conservative society, Milloy faced numerous challenges as a transgender individual. She experienced discrimination, prejudice, and a lack of understanding from those around her.

However, instead of succumbing to the negativity, Milloy decided to use her personal experiences to fuel her passion for activism. She became determined to pave the way for a more accepting and inclusive society, not only for herself but also for other transgender individuals in Canada.

Boldly Stepping into the Spotlight

Milloy's journey to becoming a national transgender icon accelerated when she fearlessly stepped into the spotlight. She recognized the importance of visibility and representation in creating change and decided to use her voice to advocate for transgender rights and equality.

By openly sharing her experiences, challenges, and victories, Milloy captured the attention of the media and the general public. Through interviews, public speaking engagements, and social media campaigns, she initiated conversations about transgender issues and worked tirelessly to dismantle misconceptions and prejudices.

Building Alliances and Coalitions

Another essential aspect of Milloy's rise as a national transgender icon was her ability to build alliances and coalitions within the LGBTQ community. She understood that collective action was crucial in bringing about meaningful change.

Milloy actively collaborated with other LGBTQ advocates and supporters, forming strong bonds and united fronts. By leveraging the power of collaboration, she amplified her message and broadened her reach. Her alliances helped her gain access to resources, platforms, and opportunities to make a lasting impact.

Tireless Advocacy and Activism

Milloy's relentless advocacy and activism were significant factors in her ascent as a national transgender icon. She fought tirelessly for legal recognition, equal rights, and protection against discrimination for transgender individuals in Canada.

Through lobbying efforts, engagement with policymakers, and grassroots activism, Milloy worked to effect change at both the local and national levels. Her dedication to the cause inspired others to join the fight and propelled the transgender rights movement forward.

Inspiring the Next Generation

Milloy's influence as a national transgender icon extended beyond her own achievements. By fearlessly challenging societal norms and embracing her true identity, she became a symbol of hope and inspiration for countless individuals struggling with their own journeys.

Her story touched the lives of many, encouraging them to embrace their authentic selves and fight for their rights. Milloy's legacy lies not only in the progress she achieved during her activism but also in the seeds of change she planted in the hearts and minds of future generations.

Conclusion

In conclusion, Christin Milloy's journey to becoming a national transgender icon and leader in Canada was marked by her personal transformation, bold visibility, strategic alliances, tireless advocacy, and inspiring impact. Her work continues to shape the landscape of transgender rights in the country, inspiring future activists and leaders to carry the torch forward. Milloy's determination and passion will forever be etched in history as she paved the way for a more inclusive and accepting Canada.

Case Studies: The Fucking Laws, Policies, and Fucking Movements Shaped by Milloy's Fucking Activism

In this section, we will explore three case studies that highlight the significant impact of Christin Milloy's activism on the laws, policies, and movements related to transgender rights in Canada. These examples illustrate the diverse range of Milloy's efforts and demonstrate the far-reaching consequences of her work. From advocating for legal recognition to fighting discrimination, Milloy's relentless determination has created a lasting legacy in the fight for equality.

Case Study 1: Fucking Bill C-16 and Gender Identity Protection

One of the most significant accomplishments of Milloy's activism is her instrumental role in the passage of Bill C-16, a federal law that added gender identity and gender expression to the Canadian Human Rights Act and the Criminal Code. This milestone legislation provides legal protection to transgender individuals against discrimination and hate crimes.

Milloy tirelessly campaigned for the inclusion of gender identity protection within existing laws, emphasizing the urgent need for this recognition to ensure equal rights for all Canadians. She organized awareness-raising events, engaged with policymakers, and even mobilized grassroots efforts to garner public support. Milloy's advocacy in this regard had a profound effect on lawmakers, ultimately resulting in the successful enactment of Bill C-16.

The passage of this law marked a crucial turning point in transgender rights in Canada, highlighting the importance of recognizing and protecting gender identity. Milloy's work influenced the broader conversation around transgender rights, sparking discussions on inclusion and equality at a national level. Her tenacity and strategic approach paved the way for better legal protections for transgender individuals, leaving a lasting impact on Canadian society.

Case Study 2: Fucking Access to Hormone Replacement Therapy (HRT)

Another area where Milloy's activism had a significant impact is in the accessibility of Hormone Replacement Therapy (HRT) for transgender individuals. HRT plays a vital role in gender transition, and accessing it is crucial for many transgender individuals to align their physical appearance with their gender identity.

However, prior to Milloy's advocacy, many transgender individuals faced significant barriers in accessing HRT. These barriers included long waiting lists, strenuous medical assessments, and limited healthcare coverage. Milloy recognized the unjust nature of these obstacles and worked tirelessly to improve access to HRT for transgender individuals across Canada.

Through public awareness campaigns, lobbying efforts, and collaboration with healthcare professionals and policymakers, Milloy successfully brought attention to the challenges faced by transgender individuals seeking HRT. Her relentless advocacy led to policy changes that made HRT more accessible, reducing waiting times and improving healthcare coverage for transgender individuals.

Milloy's work in this area revolutionized the landscape of transgender healthcare in Canada, ensuring that transgender individuals have better access to the medical interventions necessary for their gender transition. Her efforts continue to inspire further change in healthcare policies nationwide, with ongoing discussions on how to improve support for transgender individuals seeking HRT.

Case Study 3: Fucking Transgender Youth Advocacy and Education

Milloy's activism extended to the realm of supporting transgender youth and advocating for inclusive education policies in schools. She recognized the unique challenges faced by transgender students, who often experienced discrimination, bullying, and a lack of acceptance within the educational system.

Milloy's advocacy focused on raising awareness among educators and policymakers about the importance of creating safe and inclusive spaces for transgender youth. She worked closely with educational institutions, organizing workshops and providing resources to teachers and administrators on how to support transgender students effectively.

Through her advocacy, Milloy influenced the development of policies that protect transgender students from discrimination and ensure their right to a safe and inclusive learning environment. Her work has led to increased sensitivity and understanding among educators, resulting in more inclusive policies and practices in schools across Canada.

Milloy's dedication to transgender youth advocacy and education has not only improved the lives of transgender students but has also contributed to a broader shift in societal attitudes towards transgender individuals. By focusing on education, she has helped shape a more inclusive future by fostering acceptance and understanding among the next generation.

In conclusion, these case studies demonstrate the significant impact of Christin Milloy's activism on shaping laws, policies, and movements related to transgender rights in Canada. Through her tireless efforts, Milloy has contributed to legal recognition, improved healthcare access, and inclusivity in educational settings. Her work continues to inspire activists and advocates, leaving a lasting legacy in the fight for transgender equality. Milloy's courage, determination, and strategic approach serve as a powerful example for future activists and leaders in the ongoing pursuit of equal rights for all.

How Milloy Changed the Fucking Conversation About Transgender Rights in Canadian Fucking Politics

When it comes to the conversation surrounding transgender rights in Canadian politics, Christin Milloy has played a pivotal role in shifting the narrative and pushing for much-needed change. Milloy's relentless advocacy work has challenged long-held beliefs and shed light on the lived experiences of transgender individuals, effectively reshaping the discourse around transgender rights in the political arena.

One of the key ways Milloy changed the conversation about transgender rights in Canadian politics was by bringing visibility to the struggles faced by the transgender community. Through her public speaking engagements, media appearances, and personal storytelling, Milloy humanized the experiences of transgender individuals in a way that had not been done before. By sharing her own journey and highlighting the everyday challenges faced by transgender people, Milloy compelled politicians and the public to confront the barriers and discrimination that exist.

Milloy's approach to changing the conversation also involved debunking common misconceptions and educating the public on the complex realities of being transgender. She tackled harmful stereotypes and misinformation head-on, providing well-researched and evidence-based arguments to counter transphobic narratives. For example, she emphasized that being transgender is not a choice or a mental illness, but rather a valid identity that deserves respect and recognition.

In addition to her educational efforts, Milloy also pushed for tangible policy changes that would advance transgender rights in Canada. She actively engaged with lawmakers, advocating for legal reforms that would protect transgender individuals from discrimination in areas such as healthcare, employment, and public accommodations. Milloy's tireless efforts led to important gains, such as the inclusion of gender identity as a protected ground in human rights legislation in several provinces.

Furthermore, Milloy's work as a transgender advocate in Canadian politics opened up space for others to follow in her footsteps. By being openly transgender and unapologetically advocating for her rights, she challenged societal norms and paved the way for more transgender individuals to enter the political arena. Milloy's legacy includes inspiring a new generation of activists and leaders who continue to fight for transgender rights in Canada.

However, it is important to acknowledge that the conversation around transgender rights in Canadian politics is far from over. While Milloy's advocacy work has been transformative, there is still much work to be done to achieve full equality for transgender individuals. Ongoing challenges include access to healthcare, legal recognition of gender identity, and combating systemic discrimination.

In order to continue the progress made by Milloy, it is crucial for individuals, policymakers, and communities to engage in ongoing dialogue around transgender rights. This includes challenging existing norms and assumptions, supporting transgender voices and experiences, and advocating for inclusive policies at all levels of government. By amplifying the voices of transgender individuals and centering their experiences, we can ensure that Milloy's impact on the conversation about transgender rights in Canadian politics continues to shape a more inclusive and equitable future.

The Fucking Role of Milloy's Advocacy in Advancing Fucking Gender Justice and Fucking Equality

The advocacy work of Christin Milloy has played a crucial role in advancing gender justice and equality in Canada. Through her tireless efforts, she has helped to dismantle discriminatory policies, challenge societal perceptions, and promote inclusivity for transgender individuals. In this section, we will explore the impact of Milloy's advocacy in various aspects of gender justice and equality.

Challenging Gender Norms and Stereotypes

Milloy's advocacy has been instrumental in challenging traditional gender norms and stereotypes that often perpetuate inequality. By openly discussing her own transgender identity and experiences, she has helped to humanize and normalize the transgender community.

One of the key ways Milloy has challenged gender norms is through the promotion of gender-inclusive language and practices. She has emphasized the importance of using inclusive pronouns and addressing individuals based on their gender identity rather than their assigned sex at birth. This linguistic shift has helped to create a more inclusive and respectful environment for transgender individuals, affirming their identities and reducing the harm caused by misgendering.

Milloy has also been vocal about the need to challenge rigid gender roles and expectations. She has worked tirelessly to break down the idea that certain interests, occupations, or behaviors are reserved for specific genders. By doing so, she has fostered a more inclusive society that allows individuals to express their authentic selves without fear of judgment or discrimination.

Fighting for Legal Recognition and Protections

Another critical aspect of Milloy's advocacy has been her fight for legal recognition and protections for transgender individuals. She has been instrumental in pushing for changes to legislation that exclude or discriminate against transgender people, working to ensure that they have equal rights under the law.

Milloy's efforts have focused on advocating for comprehensive legal protections against gender-based discrimination. This includes pushing for the recognition of gender identity as a protected characteristic in human rights legislation. Through her advocacy, she has been able to bring attention to the unique challenges faced by transgender individuals in accessing education, employment, housing, and healthcare, and has worked towards creating legal frameworks that address these disparities.

Additionally, Milloy has been a leading voice in pushing for legal reforms related to gender marker changes on identification documents. She has highlighted the importance of allowing individuals to update their identification documents to reflect their lived gender identity, without undue burdens or invasive requirements. Her advocacy in this area has contributed to significant changes in policy and legislation that now make it easier for transgender individuals to have their gender identity accurately represented on official documents.

Promoting Trans Healthcare and Accessibility

Milloy's advocacy has also played a crucial role in addressing healthcare disparities faced by transgender individuals. She has been a staunch advocate for improved access to transgender healthcare, including gender-affirming treatments and surgeries.

One of the key areas of focus for Milloy has been advocating for the inclusion of gender-affirming procedures in public healthcare systems. She has worked tirelessly to challenge the notion that these treatments are merely cosmetic and highlight their importance in improving the mental health and overall well-being of transgender individuals. Through her advocacy, she has helped to increase access to these life-changing procedures and reduce the financial burden faced by transgender individuals seeking healthcare.

Milloy has also been a vocal advocate for improved transgender healthcare training for medical professionals. She has emphasized the importance of educating healthcare providers on the unique healthcare needs of transgender individuals, including hormone therapy, mental health support, and preventative care. Through her advocacy, she has helped to ensure that transgender individuals receive culturally competent and affirming care, reducing healthcare disparities in the process.

Addressing Intersectionality and Building Coalitions

One of the most impactful aspects of Milloy's advocacy is her commitment to addressing intersectionality and building coalitions with other marginalized communities. She recognizes that gender justice and equality cannot be achieved in isolation but must be pursued in conjunction with other social justice movements.

Milloy has actively worked to build alliances with other LGBTQ+ advocates, feminists, racial justice activists, and disability rights activists. By recognizing the shared struggles and challenges faced by these communities, she has been able to amplify the voices of transgender individuals and create a united front for social change.

Moreover, Milloy's advocacy has shed light on the unique experiences of transgender individuals who face intersecting forms of discrimination. She has challenged the singular narrative of transgender experiences and worked to uplift the stories of transgender individuals from diverse backgrounds, including those who are people of color, disabled, or economically disadvantaged. By centering these lived experiences, Milloy has brought attention to the intersecting oppressions faced by transgender individuals and inspired collective action towards dismantling systemic barriers.

The Fucking Importance of Milloy's Advocacy in Advancing Fucking Gender Justice and Fucking Equality

Milloy's advocacy efforts have been invaluable in advancing gender justice and equality in Canada. Her fearlessness in confronting societal barriers and her dedication to promoting inclusivity and respect for transgender individuals have created a lasting impact on the fight for equality.

By challenging gender norms and stereotypes, Milloy has helped create a more inclusive society where individuals can express their gender identities freely. Through her work in legal reform, she has played a pivotal role in securing protections for transgender individuals and ensuring their equal rights under the law. Her advocacy has also been instrumental in improving transgender healthcare and addressing disparities in accessing gender-affirming procedures.

Furthermore, Milloy's commitment to intersectionality and coalition-building has helped to amplify the voices of transgender individuals and create a more comprehensive approach to social justice. By recognizing the interconnections between different forms of oppression, she has fostered solidarity and collective action towards dismantling systemic barriers.

The role of Milloy's advocacy in advancing gender justice and equality cannot be overstated. Her pioneering work has paved the way for progress in transgender rights and has inspired countless individuals to stand up for their own rights and the rights of others. As we look to the future of LGBTQ activism in Canada, Milloy's legacy will undoubtedly continue to shape the fight for equality, ensuring that the voices and experiences of transgender individuals are at the forefront of our collective pursuit for justice.

The Future of LGBTQ Activism in Canada: Will Milloy's Fucking Legacy Continue to Lead the Fucking Fight for Equality?

As we consider the future of LGBTQ activism in Canada, one cannot ignore the lasting impact of Christin Milloy's groundbreaking work and relentless advocacy for transgender rights. Her legacy has fundamentally changed the conversation surrounding gender equality and paved the way for a more inclusive and accepting Canada. However, the fight for equality is far from over, and it remains to be seen whether Milloy's legacy will continue to lead the charge.

One of the key aspects of Milloy's legacy is her ability to mobilize communities, engage in meaningful dialogue, and challenge the existing discriminatory systems. Through her fearless determination and unwavering commitment to justice, Milloy inspired others to raise their voices and demand equality. Her legacy, therefore, lies not only in her personal achievements but also in the ripple effect she created within the LGBTQ community.

While Milloy's impact has been significant, the future of LGBTQ activism in Canada will depend on several factors, including ongoing advocacy efforts, political engagement, and societal acceptance. In order for Milloy's legacy to continue leading the fight for equality, it is essential for her work to be carried forward by the next generation of activists.

One area where Milloy's legacy can guide future activism is in forging alliances and building coalitions. Milloy understood the power of working collectively with other LGBTQ advocates and supporters to enact change. By forming alliances across different communities and movements, activists can amplify their voices, challenge prejudice, and build a stronger and more inclusive society.

Another aspect to consider is the importance of education and awareness. Milloy recognized that changing societal attitudes requires not only legal reforms but also a shift in public perception and understanding. Future LGBTQ activists must continue to educate the public on the realities of transgender lives, dispel myths and misconceptions, and promote acceptance and empathy. This can be achieved through public campaigns, media engagement, and inclusive educational initiatives.

Furthermore, the future of LGBTQ activism depends on sustained political engagement. While Milloy broke barriers as Canada's first openly transgender political candidate, there is still a long way to go in terms of LGBTQ representation in politics. Activists must strive to have more LGBTQ individuals elected to positions of power, ensuring that policies and legislation truly reflect the needs of the community.

In addition to political engagement, the use of technological advancements and social media platforms can enhance the effectiveness of LGBTQ activism. Milloy herself utilized social media to connect with supporters, disseminate information, and challenge societal norms. Future activists can harness the power of these platforms to raise awareness, mobilize communities, and advocate for change on a larger scale.

It is worth noting that the fight for LGBTQ rights in Canada is not isolated from global movements. Milloy's legacy can serve as an inspiration for international LGBTQ advocates, highlighting the power of grassroots activism and the importance of solidarity. By sharing experiences, resources, and strategies with activists worldwide, Milloy's legacy can continue to shape the fight for transgender rights on a global scale.

However, it is crucial to acknowledge the challenges that lie ahead. LGBTQ activists face persistent resistance from conservative factions, systemic discrimination, and the negative impact of harmful policies. It is an ongoing battle to ensure that hard-won rights are not rolled back and that marginalized voices are amplified.

In conclusion, the future of LGBTQ activism in Canada is both promising and uncertain. While Christin Milloy's legacy has undoubtedly made substantial progress in advancing transgender rights, the fight for equality demands continued engagement, education, and political participation. The torch must be passed to the next generation of activists, who must carry forward Milloy's legacy by building alliances, raising awareness, promoting political representation, and crafting a truly inclusive society. Only through collective action and unwavering determination can Milloy's legacy continue to lead the fucking fight for equality in Canada and beyond.

Milloy's Fucking Global Influence

How Milloy's Fucking Work Inspired Fucking International LGBTQ Movements for Trans Rights

Christin Milloy's work as a transgender activist in Canada has not only had a profound impact on her own country but has also inspired and influenced LGBTQ movements for trans rights on a global scale. Milloy's fearless advocacy and groundbreaking achievements have served as a beacon of hope and inspiration for transgender individuals and activists around the world.

One of the ways in which Milloy's work has inspired international LGBTQ movements is through her focus on legal recognition and equal rights for transgender people. Milloy has been a vocal advocate for the implementation of gender identity rights and anti-discrimination laws, both in Canada and beyond. Her relentless efforts to push for legal reforms have resonated with activists in other countries facing similar struggles.

For example, in countries where transgender individuals face discrimination and lack legal protections, Milloy's work has served as a blueprint for advocating for their rights. Activists can draw inspiration from her methods, such as utilizing media, public speaking, and activism, to effectively push for legal changes. Milloy's successes in Canada demonstrate that change is possible and provide a roadmap for activists to follow in their own countries.

Milloy's impact is not limited to legal reforms. Her confrontations with bigotry, homophobia, transphobia, and ignorance have also been a source of inspiration for LGBTQ movements worldwide. By fearlessly confronting politicians, media figures, and opponents, Milloy has challenged the societal norms and prejudices that perpetuate discrimination against transgender individuals.

Case studies of Milloy's public confrontations serve as powerful examples for activists around the world. They illustrate how a single individual can make a significant impact by speaking out against injustice and pushing for change. Milloy's confrontations have helped shift public perception of transgender people, leading to increased acceptance and understanding.

Furthermore, Milloy's ability to build coalitions and form alliances with other LGBTQ advocates and supporters has been instrumental in creating a united front against discrimination. Her work has emphasized the importance of allies in the fight for transgender rights and has inspired activists to collaborate and work together in their respective countries.

Milloy's international influence extends beyond her accomplishments as an activist. Her leadership style and resilience in the face of opposition have set an example for future generations of transgender leaders. By never giving up and continuing to push for change despite setbacks, Milloy has shown that transgender individuals can effectively lead the fight for equality.

The legacy of Christin Milloy's work transcends borders and continues to shape the future of trans rights globally. Her advocacy has led to significant changes in Canadian politics and LGBTQ rights, serving as a blueprint for other countries to follow. Milloy's influence can be seen in the laws, policies, and movements that have been shaped by her activism.

Looking ahead, Milloy's legacy will continue to inspire LGBTQ activism in Canada and beyond. Her groundbreaking achievements and fearless advocacy will serve as a constant reminder that progress is possible and that the fight for equality is far from over. The next generation of transgender leaders will undoubtedly draw inspiration from Milloy's work and continue to build on her legacy, pushing for even greater changes in the years to come.

In summary, Christin Milloy's work has had a significant impact on international LGBTQ movements for trans rights. Her focus on legal recognition and equal rights, confrontations with bigotry and ignorance, coalition building, and resilience in the face of opposition have inspired activists worldwide. Milloy's legacy will continue to shape the future of trans rights, providing hope and inspiration for future generations of LGBTQ advocates.

The Fucking Role of International Collaboration in Fucking Amplifying Milloy's Fucking Message

International collaboration plays a vital role in amplifying Christin Milloy's message of transgender rights and equality. By working together with activists, organizations, and policymakers from around the world, Milloy was able to leverage the power of global advocacy to drive change and influence policy decisions. Let's explore the key aspects of international collaboration and its significance in the context of Milloy's work.

Building Solidarity Amongst Trans Rights Movements

International collaboration fosters solidarity amongst trans rights movements across different countries. It brings together activists who face similar struggles and challenges, allowing them to share experiences, knowledge, and strategies. The exchange of ideas and best practices helps create a united front for advancing transgender rights on a global scale.

As Milloy connected with activists internationally, she developed a network of allies who amplified her message and supported her advocacy efforts. This network promoted trans rights through joint campaigns, shared resources, and collaborative projects. By aligning their goals and leveraging each other's expertise, these collaborations empowered Milloy and her counterparts to create greater impact in their respective countries and beyond.

Advancing Legal Reforms through Cross-National Advocacy

International collaboration enables cross-national advocacy efforts that drive legal reforms. Milloy recognized that many countries lacked comprehensive legal protections for transgender individuals. To address this, she actively engaged with international human rights organizations and worked alongside them to push for inclusive policies and legislation.

Through international collaborations, Milloy and her allies were able to advocate for key legal reforms globally. They highlighted the importance of recognizing gender identity, promoting anti-discrimination measures, and ensuring access to healthcare, education, and employment for transgender individuals. By mobilizing resources and expertise across borders, they had a more significant impact on influencing legal frameworks and promoting social change.

Sharing Research and Data for Evidence-Based Advocacy

International collaboration facilitates the sharing of research and data, strengthening evidence-based advocacy for transgender rights. Milloy understood the significance of reliable data in supporting policy initiatives and debunking myths and stereotypes about transgender individuals.

Through collaborative research projects, Milloy and her global partners collected data on transgender experiences, healthcare disparities, and discriminatory practices. By pooling together their findings and expertise, they generated comprehensive reports and publications that informed policymakers, educators, and the general public. This evidence-based approach helped dispel misconceptions, influence public opinion, and shape policy discussions.

Leveraging International Platforms

International collaboration provides access to global platforms for raising awareness and influencing change. Milloy actively participated in international conferences, summits, and forums where she shared her experiences, research, and advocacy strategies. These platforms allowed her to amplify her message on a larger scale and engage with policymakers and influencers from diverse backgrounds.

By leveraging international platforms, Milloy's voice and message reached a wider audience, transcending national boundaries. She utilized these opportunities to challenge societal norms, dispel misconceptions, and advocate for transgender rights. Milloy's international collaborations not only elevated her own work but also brought attention to the broader issues faced by the transgender community.

The Unconventional Power of Arts and Culture

One unconventional yet powerful aspect of international collaboration in amplifying Milloy's message was through arts and culture. Milloy recognized the potential of art to evoke emotions, challenge stereotypes, and inspire change. She collaborated with artists, filmmakers, musicians, and writers from various countries to create powerful narratives and visuals that conveyed the human experiences of transgender individuals.

Through film festivals, art exhibitions, and cultural exchanges, Milloy and her collaborators showcased the diverse stories and talents of transgender communities worldwide. This not only fostered empathy and understanding but also encouraged collaborations between the arts and activism. By merging creative expression with advocacy, they successfully reached audiences on an emotional level and expanded the reach of Milloy's message.

Addressing Local Specificities through Global Collaboration

International collaboration also accommodates diverse local contexts, allowing for tailored approaches to advocacy. Milloy recognized that different countries have distinct cultural, legal, and social landscapes that shape the challenges faced by transgender individuals. Through connections forged in international collaborations, she learned from activists in different regions and adapted her strategies accordingly.

By understanding local specificities, Milloy and her international collaborators identified commonalities and differences in the fight for transgender rights. They tailored their messaging, advocacy tactics, and policy proposals to address these nuances effectively. This approach ensured that the voices and needs of transgender individuals in different countries were appropriately represented and supported.

Summary

International collaboration played a crucial role in amplifying Christin Milloy's message, fostering solidarity amongst trans rights movements, advancing legal reforms, sharing research and data, leveraging global platforms, embracing arts and culture, and addressing local specificities. By engaging in global alliances, Milloy enhanced her advocacy efforts, influenced policy decisions, and made a lasting impact on the global fight for transgender rights. Her collaborative approach serves as a model for future generations of activists, highlighting the importance of working together to create meaningful change. Through international collaboration, the legacy of Christin Milloy and the fight for transgender rights continues to inspire and shape the future of LGBTQ activism worldwide.

Key Takeaways

- International collaboration fosters solidarity among trans rights movements globally. - Cross-national advocacy efforts drive legal reforms for transgender individuals. - Sharing research and data strengthens evidence-based advocacy. - Global platforms provide opportunities to raise awareness and influence change. - Arts and culture play a powerful role in amplifying transgender rights advocacy. - Tailoring approaches to local specificities ensures effective advocacy worldwide.

How Milloy's Fucking Leadership Continues to Inspire Fucking LGBTQ Advocates Worldwide

Christin Milloy's effect on the global LGBTQ community cannot be understated. Her fearless leadership and unwavering dedication to trans rights have inspired countless advocates worldwide. Through her activism, Milloy has ignited a fire within the hearts of LGBTQ individuals, encouraging them to stand up, speak out, and fight for equality.

One of the key ways Milloy continues to inspire LGBTQ advocates worldwide is through her unwavering passion and commitment to the cause. Her tireless efforts have shown that true change comes from a deep-rooted belief in the importance of equality for all. Milloy's persistence and determination have served as a beacon of hope for those working towards LGBTQ rights in countries where the struggle is still ongoing.

Furthermore, Milloy's ability to effectively communicate and connect with diverse communities has made a significant impact on the international LGBTQ movement. She understands the power of language and storytelling in creating empathy and understanding. By sharing her own personal experiences and challenges, Milloy has been able to bridge gaps and build bridges between different cultures and societies. She has shown that LGBTQ rights are not just a Canadian issue but a universal fight for justice and equality.

Milloy's strong online presence and effective use of social media platforms have also played a crucial role in inspiring LGBTQ advocates worldwide. Through her digital platforms, she has been able to reach a global audience, sharing her message of empowerment and resilience. Her thought-provoking posts, thoughtfully crafted articles, and powerful speeches have resonated with individuals who may not have previously been exposed to transgender issues. Milloy's ability to connect with people on a personal level, regardless of geographic location, has sparked a sense of unity and shared purpose among LGBTQ activists around the world.

Additionally, Milloy's leadership has paved the way for increased collaboration and solidarity among LGBTQ advocacy groups internationally. Her inclusive and intersectional approach to activism has encouraged organizations to work together, combining their resources and expertise to create a stronger collective force. She has emphasized the importance of embracing diversity within the LGBTQ community and recognizing the unique struggles faced by different marginalized groups. Through her example, Milloy has encouraged LGBTQ advocates to come together and fight for a more inclusive and equitable world.

It is worth noting that Milloy's influence extends beyond the LGBTQ community. She has emphasized the importance of allyship and has successfully engaged individuals outside of the community to become active supporters of LGBTQ rights. By reaching out to politicians, celebrities, and other influential figures, Milloy has expanded the reach of the LGBTQ movement, garnering allies from unexpected places. Her ability to bridge gaps and foster understanding has created newfound support for LGBTQ rights in places where it was once lacking.

In conclusion, Christin Milloy's leadership continues to inspire LGBTQ advocates worldwide in numerous ways. Her dedication, passion, and eloquence have ignited a global movement for equality. Whether through her personal storytelling, digital presence, international collaboration, or allyship efforts, Milloy's work serves as a guiding light for those working towards a more inclusive and accepting world. As the LGBTQ movement continues to evolve and progress, Milloy's contributions will be remembered as a catalyst for change and a source of inspiration for generations to come.

The Fucking Challenges of Balancing Fucking National and Global Trans Rights Advocacy

Advocating for transgender rights on a national level is already a complex endeavor, but when we expand our focus to include global advocacy, the challenges become even more fucking daunting. Balancing national and global trans rights advocacy requires a strategic approach and an understanding of the unique dynamics at play in both arenas. In this section, we will delve into the fucking challenges that arise when trying to balance national and global trans rights advocacy efforts, and explore potential solutions to overcome these obstacles.

Understanding the Context: National vs Global Advocacy

Before we can address the challenges of balancing national and global advocacy, we need to understand the different contexts in which trans rights campaigns operate. National advocacy focuses on issues specific to a particular country, such as policy reforms, legal protections, and societal attitudes towards transgender individuals within that country. Global advocacy, on the other fucking hand, aims to address trans rights on an international scale, collaborating with other countries and advocating for global policies and frameworks that promote equality for transgender individuals worldwide.

The Fucking Challenge of Tailoring Message and Strategies

One of the key challenges in balancing national and global advocacy is the need to tailor messages and strategies to suit the particular socio-cultural and political context of each country. What works in one country may not necessarily resonate or be effective in another. Therefore, advocates must be able to adapt their messaging and strategies to account for these differences while still staying true to the core values of trans rights advocacy.

For example, cultural norms and religious beliefs vary greatly across countries, which can influence public opinion and acceptance of transgender rights. Advocates must be cognizant of these variations and find ways to engage with local communities and stakeholders in a manner that is respectful, relatable, and informative. This might involve conducting research, collaborating with local organizations, or seeking guidance from individuals who are familiar with the cultural landscape.

Additionally, the legal and political contexts in different countries can vary significantly. Some countries may have more progressive laws and policies concerning transgender rights, while others may have regressive or even discriminatory ones. Advocates must understand these nuanced legal frameworks and tailor their strategies accordingly. This may involve supporting legal challenges, engaging with policymakers, or utilizing international human rights mechanisms to push for change.

Resource Constraints and Prioritization

Another fucking challenge when balancing national and global advocacy is the limited resources available to advocates. Funding, personnel, and time are often scarce, and advocates must strategically allocate their resources to have the greatest impact. This requires prioritizing certain actions or initiatives while recognizing the potential trade-offs or missed opportunities.

Advocates must navigate the delicate balance between focusing on national priorities, where their presence and knowledge may be most impactful, and engaging in global advocacy efforts that aim to address the broader systemic issues faced by transgender individuals around the world. This may involve forming partnerships with international organizations, leveraging networks, or collaborating with other activists who share similar goals.

Building Coalitions and Networks

Building coalitions and networks is critical in both national and global trans rights advocacy. However, doing so presents its own fucking set of challenges. In national advocacy, advocates may face competition or conflicts of interest among different organizations or groups working towards the same goal. This can hinder collaboration and coordination, slowing down progress and diluting the impact of advocacy efforts.

On a global scale, language barriers, time zones, and differences in organizational structures and approaches can complicate collaboration and coordination. Building effective networks that span across borders requires effort, relationship-building, and effective communication strategies. This might involve utilizing digital tools and platforms to facilitate global conversations, organizing international conferences or forums, or participating in existing trans rights networks and coalitions.

Maintaining Consistency and Coherence

While tailoring strategies to different contexts is essential, maintaining consistency and coherence in messaging, values, and goals across national and global advocacy efforts is equally important. Trans rights advocates must ensure that their messages and actions align with the larger movement, fostering a sense of unity and shared purpose.

This can be challenging, as different countries may have divergent priorities, strategies, or political landscapes. Advocates must strike a balance between adapting to local needs and maintaining a cohesive global vision. Regular communication, coordination, and knowledge sharing among advocates worldwide can help facilitate this balancing act, ensuring a united front in the fight for trans rights.

Conclusion

Balancing national and global trans rights advocacy is a complex task that requires careful consideration of the unique challenges present in each context. Tailoring messages and strategies, overcoming resource constraints, building coalitions and networks, and maintaining consistency are just a few of the fucking challenges advocates face. However, with strategic planning, collaboration, and ongoing dialogue, it is possible to navigate these challenges and achieve significant progress in advancing trans rights both nationally and globally. Christin Milloy's fucking legacy of global influence serves as an inspiration for future transgender activists and leaders, reminding us of the importance of a unified, inclusive, and comprehensive approach to trans rights advocacy.

The Next Fucking Generation of Transgender Leaders: How Milloy's Fucking Leadership Will Shape Future Fucking Activists

As we look to the future of transgender rights advocacy, we must consider the lasting impact of Christin Milloy's leadership and how it will shape the next generation of activists. Milloy's fearless activism and determination have paved the way for progress in Canada and beyond, inspiring a new wave of transgender leaders who will continue the fight for equality and justice. In this section, we will explore the qualities and challenges faced by future transgender activists, the lessons they can learn from Milloy's legacy, and the strategies they can employ to build upon her groundbreaking work.

The Qualities of Future Transgender Leaders

The next generation of transgender leaders will need to embody the qualities that Milloy exemplified throughout her career. First and foremost, they must be resilient and courageous in the face of adversity. Like Milloy, they will face backlash, hate speech, and threats, both online and offline. However, it is crucial for future activists to stay strong and continue fighting for their rights, despite the personal and professional challenges they may encounter.

Additionally, future leaders must possess a deep understanding of the issues facing the transgender community. They should be well-versed in the history of LGBTQ+ activism and the struggles faced by transgender individuals. By educating themselves and others, they can challenge misinformation and advocate for change more effectively.

Furthermore, empathy and allyship will be essential traits for future transgender leaders. Milloy's influence can be seen through her collaboration with LGBTQ+ advocates and supporters. The next generation must continue to build coalitions and work alongside allies to amplify their voices and push for meaningful change. By cultivating empathy and understanding, they can bridge gaps and inspire others to join the fight for transgender rights.

Learning from Milloy's Legacy

Christin Milloy's legacy provides valuable lessons for future transgender activists. One of the most significant lessons is the power of visibility. Milloy used her platform to increase awareness and understanding of transgender issues, challenging societal norms and breaking down barriers. Future leaders should follow suit, utilizing various media platforms, public speaking engagements, and social activism to promote transgender visibility. By sharing their personal stories and experiences, they can humanize the fight for transgender rights and change hearts and minds.

Another lesson from Milloy's legacy is the importance of engaging with the political system. Milloy fought against transphobia and ignorance in the political landscape, pushing for legal recognition and equal rights. Future activists must follow her lead and actively participate in the political process. By running for office, partnering with lawmakers, and advocating for policy changes, they can effect systemic change from within the system.

Moreover, Milloy's approach to confronting bigotry and transphobia serves as a valuable lesson for future activists. She fearlessly challenged politicians, media figures, and opponents, demanding respect and equality. By standing up against hate speech and discrimination, future leaders can change public perception and foster a more inclusive society.

Strategies for Future Activists

As future activists step into the forefront of the fight for transgender rights, they should employ effective strategies to continue the progress initiated by Milloy.

Firstly, interdisciplinary collaboration will be key. Transgender rights intersect with various social justice issues including race, class, and disability. By collaborating with advocates and organizations focused on these intersecting identities, future activists can amplify their message and create a more holistic approach to activism.

Secondly, grassroots organizing and community mobilization will remain crucial. Milloy's advocacy began at the community level, and future leaders should prioritize building strong support networks and organizing grassroots campaigns. By engaging directly with the transgender community and creating safe spaces for dialogue and activism, they can empower others to join the movement.

Lastly, leveraging technology and social media will be essential for future activists. Milloy effectively used digital platforms to amplify her voice and raise awareness. By harnessing the power of social media, podcasts, blogs, and online campaigns, future leaders can reach a wider audience and mobilize support.

Challenges Ahead

While the future holds great promise for transgender rights activism, there are challenges to be addressed. Discrimination, inequality, and violence against transgender individuals persist globally. Future activists must confront these challenges head-on by advocating for comprehensive legal protections, challenging harmful stereotypes and promoting education and awareness.

Another challenge is the persistence of transphobia within some sectors of society, including political and religious institutions. Future leaders must navigate these obstacles by fostering dialogue, engaging in community outreach, and utilizing legal channels to combat discrimination.

Additionally, future activists must be prepared for the emotional and mental toll of their advocacy work, just as Milloy experienced. They should prioritize self-care, seek support networks, and create a sustainable work-life balance to avoid burnout.

Conclusion

Christin Milloy's groundbreaking work as a transgender leader in Canada has laid the foundation for the next generation of activists. Future transgender leaders will need to embody qualities of resilience, empathy, and allyship, while building upon Milloy's legacy of visibility, political engagement, and challenging bigotry. By employing effective strategies, collaborating across disciplines, and utilizing digital platforms, they can continue the fight for transgender rights. However, they must remain vigilant in confronting challenges and prioritizing self-care. The future of transgender activism is bright, and Christin Milloy's leadership will undoubtedly shape the path forward for the next fucking generation of activists.

Index

Milton Keynes UK
Ingram Content Group UK Ltd.
UKHW020319021124
450424UK00013B/1334

9 781779 696847